"Once again, Fr. Tu
that each parish an
the rituals around t
masterfully weaves .   ....., ...ui ɡy,
and reflection questions to assist the parish team's planning and
guide our understanding of 'church.' Even if we are not planning a
dedication or rededication, we are called to take time to remember
the symbols of our church buildings and altars. We are the church,
and these theological reflections guide us to be the 'solid rock' upon
which the foundation of future generations have their faith inspired."

> —Reverend John Thomas Lane, SSS, Saint Paschal Baylon
> Roman Catholic Church, Highland Heights, Ohio;
> Liturgical Consultant, Congregation of
> the Blessed Sacrament

"This book is a great example of liturgical catechesis. It can be
used in a variety of pastoral settings. It is a must-read for parishes
not only engaged in a process of building a worship space but
also renovating or simply refreshing a space. Rev. Paul Turner
puts forward a mystagogical structure highlighting the scriptural
foundation of the rites, the liturgical actions, and reflective
questions. These characteristics of faith formation deepen full,
conscious active participation not only in the rites but is attentive
to the movements of the heart."

> —Sister Sandra DeMasi, SSJ, Director of Liturgy, St. Rose of
> Lima Parish, New Jersey

Our Church, Our Altar

A People's Guide to the Dedication of a Church and Its Anniversary

Paul Turner

LITURGICAL PRESS
Collegeville, Minnesota

www.litpress.org

Cover design by Monica Bokinskie. Photograph courtesy of Dreamstime.

Scripture quotations are from New Revised Standard Version Bible © 1989 National Council of the Churches of Christ in the United States of America. Used by permission. All rights reserved worldwide.

The translation of the psalms are from *The Abbey Psalms and Canticles* by the Monks of Conception Abbey © 2019 United States Conference of Catholic Bishops, Washington, DC. All Rights Reserved.

The English translation of Psalm Responses from *Lectionary for Mass* © 1969, 1981, 1997, International Commission on English in the Liturgy Corporation (ICEL); excerpts from the English translation of *The Roman Missal* © 2010, ICEL; excerpts from the English translation of *The Order of the Dedication of a Church and an Altar* © 2014, ICEL. All rights reserved.

© 2021 by Paul Turner
Published by Liturgical Press, Collegeville, Minnesota. All rights reserved. No part of this book may be used or reproduced in any manner whatsoever, except brief quotations in reviews, without written permission of Liturgical Press, Saint John's Abbey, PO Box 7500, Collegeville, MN 56321-7500. Printed in the United States of America.

1   2   3   4   5   6   7   8   9

Library of Congress Cataloging-in-Publication Data

Names: Turner, Paul, author.
Title: Our church, our altar : a people's guide to the dedication of a church and its anniversary / Paul Turner.
Description: Collegeville, Minnesota : Liturgical Press, [2021] | Summary: "A guide for preparing the parish community to celebrate the dedication of a new church and altar and other related rituals. Includes spiritual reflections for group or individual meditation based on the biblical passages upon which the rituals rely"— Provided by publisher.
Identifiers: LCCN 2021016775 (print) | LCCN 2021016776 (ebook) | ISBN 9780814666616 (paperback) | ISBN 9780814666623 (epub) | ISBN 9780814666623 (mobi) | ISBN 9780814666623 (pdf)
Subjects: LCSH: Church dedication—Liturgy. | Altars. | Catholic Church. Dedication of a church and an altar. | Catholic Church—Liturgy.
Classification: LCC BX2302 .T87 2021 (print) | LCC BX2302 (ebook) | DDC 265/.9—dc23
LC record available at https://lccn.loc.gov/2021016775
LC ebook record available at https://lccn.loc.gov/2021016776

Contents

Introduction

We may encounter God anywhere, but we set aside special places and objects for prayer. These gain importance through their repeated, communal use from one generation to the next. They are holy not just because one person says so, but because a community of people shares the experience from age to age.

Some places become holy because of unplanned events that happened there: the sudden revelation of natural beauty, falling in love with another person, or an unexpected death. These places shimmer with divine presence because they became sacred almost of their own accord.

Other places are constructed for the purposes of prayer. A new church, for example, requires land, building, and objects that will become places of encounter with God. For these to shimmer with divine presence, deliberate actions make them sacred. In the Catholic tradition, a bishop approves construction based on the needs of the local congregation, and he presides over the ceremonies that dedicate the new sacred space.

The Vatican's Congregation for Divine Worship and the Discipline of the Sacraments approves ceremonies that pertain to dedication, gathering them into a single liturgical book called *The Order of the Dedication of a Church and an Altar*. Most parishes do not own a copy because it is used rarely. Most people have never seen it because it pertains primarily to the ministry of a bishop. And yet, when a bishop dedicates a new church, this book reminds him to assemble the people. Their pastor is to prepare them for this day.

This book will help you reflect on your church and altar, especially if they are brand new. Nonetheless, if your church was built some time ago, you may still benefit from praying about the ceremonies of its founding. Each year your parish celebrates the anniversary of its dedication. This book will help you celebrate that day as well.

The Vatican's ritual book is divided into seven chapters that cover a variety of circumstances. No one parish celebrates all seven rituals, but it occasionally needs the book for the few chapters that apply to its circumstances.

If your parish is constructing an entirely new building, then the bishop will preside over Chapters I and II: The Order of Laying a Foundation Stone or the Commencement of Work on the Building of a Church and The Order of the Dedication of a Church. That second chapter includes the dedication of the new church's new altar.

If your parish has been celebrating Mass in a building that the bishop has not yet dedicated, then he eventually comes to preside over Chapter III: The Order of the Dedication of a Church in Which Sacred Celebrations Are Already Regularly Taking Place.

If your parish is keeping its dedicated building, but replacing its altar with a new one, then the bishop uses Chapter IV: The Order of the Dedication of an Altar.

Sometimes the building set aside for worship is not a parish church but a chapel or oratory used for more restricted purposes. In that case, the bishop will preside over Chapter V: The Order of Blessing a Church. He does not "dedicate" such a church; he "blesses" it in a less solemn ceremony.

Similarly, if such a chapel or oratory receives a new altar, the bishop will bless it, not dedicate it, with the ceremonies in Chapter VI: The Order of Blessing an Altar.

Finally, if new vessels are to be set aside for the celebration of Mass, the bishop or any priest uses Chapter VII: The Order of Blessing a Chalice and a Paten.

These seven chapters appear in a book that traditionally forms part of the Roman Pontifical, the collection of ceremonies over which a bishop presides. Nonetheless, a bishop may delegate a priest to preside for them. Indeed, for a priest to dedicate a new church or a new altar, he needs a special mandate from the bishop. A priest needs no special permission, however, to bless the vessels for Mass.

Each parish celebrates the anniversary of its dedication as a solemnity each year. (References to this Mass appear in this book as "Chapter VIII.") The date calls for a special celebration of the Mass with readings and prayers. If the anniversary falls on a Sunday in Ordinary Time, it actually replaces the usual Sunday Mass.

All of these rituals derive their inspiration from multiple passages in the Bible. Some of these passages have influenced more than one of these events. Consequently, this *People's Guide* is designed to help you pray over the pertinent biblical texts. No matter which ceremonies your community will experience or has experienced in the past, these reflections will help you pray about the sacredness of the place where you worship and the principal objects in use.

Below you will find an outline of the seven ceremonies in the *Order of the Dedication*, as well as information on the anniversary celebration. Whether you are preparing for the event or reflecting on it afterward, this section will explain it. Each section lists the biblical citations that have inspired the ceremony.

The rest of this book lists those citations in biblical order, so that you may choose those that pertain to the ceremony of interest. Reading the verses from a Bible and the reflections from this book will deepen your encounter with God in the building and objects that your bishop has set aside for liturgical prayer. May you come to treasure more deeply your place as a living stone in the church.

THE
CEREMONIES

The Order of Laying a Foundation Stone or the Commencement of Work on the Building of a Church

Just before the construction on a new church begins, the parish community gathers with the bishop for prayer. This ceremony will reach its ultimate conclusion in Chapter II, the dedication of the new church with its altar. This liturgy takes place apart from Mass, largely because the church for Mass does not yet exist.

Part One: The Approach to the Place Where the Church Is to Be Built

The ceremony begins either at a distance from the building site or directly on it. If a former church or some other large room accessible to the parish stands nearby, the people may gather there first. From there, they process with the bishop to the building site. If no such place is convenient, the people gather on location where the construction is about to begin.

A wooden cross marks the place where the altar will stand, continuing a custom that has been part of this ceremony at least since the thirteenth century. The altar will be the central place where the community celebrates the sacrament of the sacrifice of Christ on the cross.

First Form: The Procession

Gathered in a suitable place and anticipating a procession, the people welcome the bishop, who greets them, explains the ceremony, invites their participation, and recites an opening prayer.

The bishop then invites all to process to the building site. All may sing an antiphon and psalm, such as "My soul is longing for the courts of the Lord" with Psalm 84.

Second Form: The Station at the Place Where the New Church Is to Be Built

If a procession seems inopportune, all gather at the building site with an acclamation such as this one, which invokes the three Persons of the Holy Trinity: "May eternal peace from the eternal God be with those gathered here. May abiding peace, the Word of the Father, be peace for the people of God. May the faithful Consoler bring peace to all nations."

As in the First Form, the bishop greets the people, explains the ceremony, invites their participation, and recites the opening prayer.

Part Two: The Reading of the Word of God

One or more readings from the Bible foster the formation of the people. This ceremony takes place outdoors, so depending on factors such as the agreeableness of the weather and of the seating, the number and length of the readings may be adjusted.

The bishop preaches a homily to explain the readings and the meaning of the rite: "Christ is the cornerstone of the Church, and the structure that is going to be built by the living Church of the faithful will be at once the house of God and the house of the People of God."

After the homily, someone may read a document about the building, signed by the bishop and by representatives of the builders and of the church. This document may then be sealed into the foundation.

Part Three: The Blessing of the Site of the New Church

For the heart of the ceremony, the bishop offers a prayer of blessing over the site. He sprinkles it with blessed water, perhaps walking around the foundations. All may sing an antiphon, such as "All your walls will be of precious stones and the towers of Jerusalem built with gems," together with verses such as ones from Psalm 48.

Part Four: The Blessing and Laying of the Foundation Stone

Not every new building comes with a foundation stone, but if this one does, the bishop blesses it. He may sprinkle the stone with blessed water. He may incense it.

As a stonemason prepares to fix the slab in place, the bishop declares the meaning of the rite and prays that Christ the cornerstone may be invoked and praised in the building to be raised upon this rock.

While the stone is set in place, all may sing an antiphon, such as "The house of the Lord is founded firmly, on solid rock."

The Concluding Rites

The bishop introduces the universal prayer, and another minister leads the petitions. All may respond with words such as "Bless and preserve your Church, O Lord."

The bishop invites all to join in the Lord's Prayer, and then he alone offers a concluding prayer. He blesses the people in the usual way, and a deacon dismisses them.

The words and actions of this ceremony rely on several biblical passages. It will help you to learn which of the readings are used. You may prepare for or reflect upon this complete order of service through the meditations on the following numbers of this book:

Biblical passage	Ceremony	Reflection number
1 Corinthians 3:9c	Introduction	92
2 Chronicles 7:1, 14	Prayer	10
Ephesians 2:19-22	Prayer	100
Hebrews 12:22	Prayer	108
Revelation 21:2	Prayer	117
Psalm 84:3, 4, 6, 8, 10, 11 and 13	Procession	30
1 Kings 5:16-32 (2-18)	Reading	6
Acts 4:8-12	Reading	87
1 Corinthians 10:1-6	Reading	94
2 Chronicles 7:16a	Reading	10
Psalm 24:1-2, 3-4ab, 5-6	Reading	19
Psalm 42–43	Reading	23
Psalm 87:1-3, 4-5, 6-7	Reading	31
Ezekiel 37:27	Reading	55
Psalm 100:2, 3, 5	Reading	34
1 Corinthians 3:11	Reading	92
Psalm 118:1-2, 16ab-17, 22-23	Reading	37

Biblical passage	Ceremony	Reflection number
Isaiah 28:16-17	Reading	47
Matthew 7:21-29	Reading	64
Matthew 16:13-18	Reading	65
Mark 12:1-12	Reading	70
Luke 6:46-49	Reading	73
Psalm 48:2-4, 9-11, 13-15	The Blessing of the Site	26
Isaiah 54:12	The Blessing of the Site	48
Daniel 2:45	The Blessing and Laying of the Foundation Stone	58
Matthew 7:24	The Blessing and Laying of the Foundation Stone	64
James 2:1	The Blessing and Laying of the Foundation Stone	110
Revelation 1:6	The Blessing and Laying of the Foundation Stone	112
Revelation 22:13	The Blessing and Laying of the Foundation Stone	120
2 Chronicles 7:1	Concluding Rites	10
Ezekiel 43:1-2, 4-7a	Concluding Rites	56
Daniel 2:45	Concluding Rites	58
Matthew 7:24	Concluding Rites	64
Ephesians 2:19-22	Concluding Rites	100
1 Peter 2:4-5	Concluding Rites	111

CHAPTER II

The Order of the Dedication of a Church

The dedication of a new church includes the dedication of its altar. Those who participate in this unique ceremony take part in a historic event of wide-ranging spiritual importance. The anniversary of this day becomes part of the parish's liturgical calendar. The dedication ceremonies are complex and impressive in their scope and meaning.

Part One: The Introductory Rites

The entrance into the new church happens in one of three different ways. People may gather with the bishop in a nearby church or in another sufficiently large room, and then process with him to the new building. Or they may gather outside the door of the church. Or, if even that is not possible, they gather inside the new church.

First Form: The Procession
In the first option, the people gather with the bishop in some nearby location from which they will process to the new building. If the relics of a saint are to be enclosed in the new altar,

these are on view where the people gather. (Relics are not required for the dedication of an altar, so some churches do not have them.)

The bishop greets the people and explains the significance of the celebration, inviting their participation. A crossbearer leads the procession to the new building. Servers do not carry incense or candles because the ceremony introduces these symbols later. If relics are carried in procession, however, ministers carrying lighted candles accompany the one walking with the relics. In the procession all may sing "Let us go rejoicing to the house of the Lord" together with Psalm 122. Another hymn may be used, but this psalm has been associated with the introductory rites at least since the thirteenth century and repeats the words of Jewish pilgrims on their way to the temple of the Lord in Jerusalem.

Outside the threshold, the procession comes to a halt. A group representing those responsible for the construction approaches the bishop. They may hand him the legal documents of possession, keys, architectural plans, or a record of the laborers. A designer may tell the bishop about the art and architecture. The bishop then asks the priest entrusted with the church to open the door.

The bishop invites all to enter, which they do behind the processional cross. All may sing Psalm 24, another pilgrimage song of the Jerusalem temple, which Christians have associated with this ceremony at least since the sixth century. With this psalm, the people command the door to open—not to receive themselves, but to receive the Lord, who will dwell in this sacred house.

The bishop goes to his chair without kissing the altar, which has not yet been dedicated. If a minister has been carrying the relics of a saint in the procession, these are arranged temporarily in the sanctuary.

Second Form: The Solemn Entrance
If there is no procession from another location to the threshold, then the people gather outside the door of the church. Ideally, even the ministers arrive from outside, rather than from inside the church. If there are relics of a saint, these are on view outside the door.

The bishop greets the people and invites their participation. All may sing the antiphon associated with the procession: "Let us go rejoicing to the house of the Lord." After all, each has traveled some distance to meet together.

Representatives may present documents and explanations to the bishop, as in the First Form. The bishop asks the priest in charge to open the door, and the bishop invites all inside. All may sing Psalm 24. As in the First Form, the bishop goes directly to his chair without kissing the altar. All others take their appropriate places.

Third Form: The Simple Entrance
If no gathering can take place outside the door, then all meet inside the church. After the faithful have gathered, the bishop and ministers process to the sanctuary, together with the relics, if there are any. All sing Psalm 122 or another appropriate chant.

The bishop greets the people. Representatives present the documents and explanations to the bishop. The bishop does not ask the priest to open the door because all are already inside.

The Blessing and Sprinkling of Water
Once the bishop has reached his chair, he invites all to join him in prayer as he blesses water. Accompanied by deacons, he walks through the church sprinkling the people, the walls, and the altar. This ceremony has two purposes: It recalls the baptism of the people, and it purifies the new building and its altar. All may sing a traditional antiphon inspired by the prophecy of

Ezekiel, either "I saw water flowing from the Temple" or, during Lent, "I will pour clean water upon you and cleanse you."

The bishop returns to his chair and prays that God will "dwell in this house of prayer" and "cleanse us who are the temple where he dwells." From the beginning, the dedication of the church constitutes a rededication of the people who are the church.

The Hymn and the Collect

All sing the Gloria, as they do on other festive occasions. Even if the ceremony takes place during Advent or Lent, its celebration calls for this hymn of praise.

The bishop invites all to pray silently. All fittingly call to mind their hopes and prayers for the usage of this building. The bishop then offers the collect. He asks God to "pour out your grace upon this place" and to "extend the gift of your help to all who call upon you." Again, the bishop prays for both the building and the people who are the church. The words of this collect are almost identical to the one offered on this occasion since at least the seventh century.

Part Two: The Liturgy of the Word

As may be expected, all sit following the collect in order to listen to the first reading in the Liturgy of the Word. Because this is the first time that the Word of God will be proclaimed in this sanctuary, a brief ceremony precedes it. Two readers and the psalmist approach the presider's chair. One of the readers carries the lectionary and hands it to the bishop. The bishop shows the book to the people and declares, "May the word of God resound always in this building, to open for you the mystery of Christ and to bring about your salvation in the Church." All answer, "Amen."

The bishop hands the book back to the first reader. As the readers and the psalmist walk to the ambo, the first reader holds the lectionary aloft for all to see.

The first reading for this Mass is always Nehemiah 8:1-4a, 5-6, 8-10. The responsorial is always Psalm 19:8-9, 10, 15, with a refrain from John 6:63c. According to Nehemiah, Ezra brought the book of the law of Moses into the view of the people, stood on a newly built wooden platform, opened the book, and read its contents to the people. That action is being repeated now for the first time in this new space. The psalm expresses the people's love for God's Word.

An appropriate second reading and gospel are also proclaimed. The bishop preaches a homily that explains the readings and the meaning of the ceremony. All recite the Creed. The universal prayer is omitted because the ceremony of dedication will open with the Litany of the Saints.

Part III: The Prayer of Dedication and the Anointings

The Litany of Supplication

The bishop invites all to join in the litany. The list may include the name of the saint from whom the new church receives its title.

The litany concludes with several petitions, as usual, but one petition is unique to this celebration: "Consecrate this church for your worship." Such an intention has been part of this litany since the thirteenth century. The words are short, but their significance is strong. The singers who lead the litany call upon God to hear the prayers led by the bishop to dedicate this building for worship.

The bishop concludes the litany with a prayer newly composed for this ceremony after the Second Vatican Council. It prays that the building may be a house of salvation and grace, and that the people may worship there in spirit and truth.

The Deposition of the Relics

If relics are to be inserted into the new altar, they are secured into place under it, not on top of it. At future celebrations, when the presider and deacon enter the sanctuary, they kiss the altar, not the relics, in order to honor Christ, not the saints. The altar is a symbol of Jesus Christ and his sacrifice. The bishop dedicates the altar to God alone.

The earliest association of altars and the relics of saints comes from the fourth-century bishop of Milan, St. Ambrose. Upon discovery of the remains of two local saints, Gervase and Protase, the people prayed overnight in the presence of their relics. The next day, Ambrose set the relics beneath the altar of the local church. Even so, the martyrs and saints do not give honor to the altar; the altar renders the burial place of the saints worthy of honor.

The practice calls to mind an image from the book of Revelation, where John sees a vision of the souls of martyrs beneath the altar of God.

To avoid any doubt concerning the relics, their authenticity must be verified. If it cannot be, the altar is dedicated without relics, which are not required for the dedication of an altar or the celebration of Mass.

All may sing an antiphon, such as "Beneath the altar of God you have been placed, O Saints of God: intercede for us before the Lord Jesus Christ," which is almost identical to an antiphon in use for this occasion since the ninth century. Another possible antiphon is "The bodies of the Saints are buried in peace and their names will live for all eternity." These may be sung with Psalm 15, another pilgrimage song to the Jerusalem temple. Its verses ask who may dwell on the Lord's holy mountain. The implied answer to the question is: the saints.

If a record of the dedication of the church has been prepared, one copy may be placed under the altar together with the relics. This record details the date of dedication, the name of the presiding bishop, the title of the church, and a description of the relics; that is, which parts of the body of which saint. The document may be signed by the bishop, the priest, and local representatives.

The bishop places the relics and the record inside the opening beneath the altar, and a stonemason seals them in place.

The Prayer of Dedication

The highlight of this part of the service is the bishop's prayer of dedication. With these words, he calls upon God to make holy the church and the altar. This lengthy prayer alludes to many biblical passages. Its most significant line is when the bishop asks God to "pour forth from heaven your sanctifying power upon this church and upon this altar."

The prayer is modeled on the one that King Solomon offered at the dedication of the temple in Jerusalem. At its conclusion, the bishop lists the intended effects of his prayer: The faithful will celebrate the Eucharist, praise will resound, the poor will find mercy, the oppressed secure true freedom, and all will be clothed with the dignity of God's children.

The Anointing of the Altar and the Walls of the Church

The bishop puts on a linen apron called a gremial, because the next part of the ceremony can get a bit messy. A minister brings him a vessel of chrism, the same oil used in the baptism of children, the sacrament of confirmation, and the ordination of priests and bishops. Among the sacramental oils in the Catholic Church, chrism is the most sacred, noted for its pleasing aroma. Only a bishop may consecrate it, and he does that only once a year in a special celebration, usually held at the cathedral, with representation from clergy and laity throughout the diocese.

The bishop prays that the anointing "may express the mystery of Christ and the Church." He pours chrism on the middle of the altar and on each of its four corners. He may then smear the oil across the entire top of the altar, the part also known by its Latin title, mensa. The title "Christ" means "Anointed One," so this anointed altar will ever serve as a symbol of Christ. The bishop may enlist the help of priests to anoint the walls of the church, which have been prepared with either four or twelve crosses and holders for candles. If priests assist, they receive chrism from the bishop. As the altar symbolizes Jesus Christ, so the walls symbolize the people of God, the living stones who are the church.

During the anointing, all may sing an antiphon, such as "Behold God's dwelling with the human race" and verses such as those from Psalm 84: "How lovely is your dwelling place, O Lord of hosts."

The practice of anointing an altar recalls an event in the Bible's first book, when Jacob poured oil upon a memorial stone to mark the place of his vision of a ladder that joined earth to heaven.

The Incensation of the Altar and the Church

The bishop ignites incense placed upon the altar. Taking a thurible, he incenses the altar, then hands the thurible to a minister who incenses the bishop, the people, and the walls of the church. Meanwhile, all may sing an antiphon such as one from the book of Revelation: "An Angel stood by the altar of the Temple holding in his hand a golden censer." Verses may come from Psalm 138, which praises God in his holy temple in the presence of angels.

Incense signifies the pleasing prayers of the faithful ascending to the throne of God. It appears frequently in biblical prayer.

The Covering of the Altar

Ministers cover the mensa with the altar cloth. In many churches, sacristans work daily behind the scenes, washing, pressing, and arranging the various cloths set upon the altar. In this ceremony, they may solemnly carry their handiwork in full view of the assembly to clothe the newly dedicated altar.

Other ministers may bring forth flowers to set around the altar, enhancing its beauty and adding more fragrance to the incensed room. Candles and a cross may be placed on or near the altar.

The Lighting of the Altar and the Church

The newly dedicated altar and church receive more visual ornamentation through the lighting of the candles. These lights serve both as a sign of rejoicing and as a symbol of evangelization. This newly dedicated building will itself proclaim the Gospel for all who seek a deeper awareness of the presence of God. The bishop therefore prays that the light of Christ may "shine brightly in the Church, that all nations may attain the fullness of truth."

All may sing an antiphon and canticle such as the one recommended from the book of Tobit, "Jerusalem, city of God, you will shine with splendid light," or from Isaiah, "Your light has come, Jerusalem: the glory of the Lord has risen upon you."

Part Four: The Liturgy of the Eucharist

The Liturgy of the Eucharist

The rest of the Mass will look familiar to most Catholics. Some of the faithful bring forward gifts of bread and wine. All may sing an antiphon such as one that repeats the words of King David, who offered his possessions to the building of the future temple in Jerusalem: "Lord God, in the simplicity of my heart I have gladly offered everything."

As the bishop approaches the altar, he kisses it. The celebrant usually performs this action at the beginning of Mass, but because the altar had not yet been dedicated, the bishop deferred the kiss until this moment. He does not incense the altar, as often happens at this time in solemn celebrations, because he has just done so.

The bishop says the prayer over the offerings, asking God that the people gathered in this holy house "may come through these mysteries to everlasting salvation."

The preface for this Mass comes from the Ambrosian Rite, an expression of the Catholic faith centered in the city of Milan, Italy. Tracing its roots to the fourth-century St. Ambrose, its most famous priest of the twentieth century was Pope Paul VI, who incorporated many prayers of the Ambrosian Rite into the missal for Roman Catholics after the Second Vatican Council. This beautiful preface praises God who created the world as the temple of his glory and who permits the faithful to set aside places for worship that foreshadow the heavenly Jerusalem. It declares that the church is the holy city built upon the chosen stones of its members, who are enlivened by the Spirit and bonded in charity.

During the eucharistic prayer, the bishop or a concelebrant adds an extra petition acknowledging the ceremony of dedication and praying for the future ministry of the church.

For the communion hymn, people may sing an antiphon and psalm, such as "My house shall be a house of prayer" or "Like shoots of the olive, may the children of the Church be gathered around the table of the Lord," together with Psalm 128. As families gather around the table at home to praise God for their blessings, so the church family gathers at the table of the Eucharist for a similar purpose.

The Inauguration of the Chapel of the Most Blessed Sacrament

If the new church has a separate chapel for the tabernacle, the bishop carries a ciborium of hosts there after communion. This action inaugurates the new chapel. The bishop speaks no words of blessing, sprinkles no blessed water, and swings no incense. Simply placing the ciborium with the Blessed Sacrament inside the tabernacle renders the new space holy.

All may sing an antiphon and psalm, such as "O Jerusalem, glorify the Lord," with Psalm 147. Jerusalem, the holy city of Solomon's temple, is the paradigm for future houses of worship, gatherings of the faithful, and hopes for a heavenly dwelling place.

Once the ciborium is placed inside the tabernacle, a minister lights a candle that will ever burn there to indicate that the Blessed Sacrament is within. From this tabernacle, ministers will carry viaticum to the dying; at this tabernacle, the faithful will draw near for private worship.

For the prayer after communion, the bishop prays that the holy gifts just received may "instill in our minds an increase of your truth, so that we may constantly adore you in your holy temple." The bishop and deacon conclude the Mass in the usual way with the blessing and dismissal.

This ceremony relies on a large number of biblical passages. It will help you to learn which readings are proclaimed at the dedication. To reflect on the meaning of the words and actions, you may pray over any of these:

Biblical passage	Ceremony	Reflection number
Genesis 28:11-18	Entrance	3
Psalm 24	Entrance	19
Psalm 68:6-7, 36	Entrance	29
Psalm 100:4	Entrance	34
Psalm 122	Entrance	39
1 Peter 2:4-5	Entrance	111

Biblical passage	Ceremony	Reflection number
Ezekiel 36:22-26	The Blessing and Sprinkling of Water	54
Ezekiel 47:1, 9	The Blessing and Sprinkling of Water	57
Romans 6:3-7, 11	The Blessing and Sprinkling of Water	90
1 Corinthians 3:16	The Blessing and Sprinkling of Water	92
1 Corinthians 6:19	The Blessing and Sprinkling of Water	93
Hebrews 12:22	The Blessing and Sprinkling of Water	108
Revelation 21:2	The Blessing and Sprinkling of Water	117
Nehemiah 8:1-4a, 5-6, 8-10	Reading	11
Psalm 19:8-9, 10, 15	Reading	17
John 6:63c	Reading	80
1 Corinthians 3:9c-11, 16-17	Reading	92
Ephesians 2:19-22	Reading	100
Hebrews 12:18-19, 22-24	Reading	108
1 Peter 2:4-5	Reading	111
2 Chronicles 7:16	Reading	10
Isaiah 66:1	Reading	52

Biblical passage	Ceremony	Reflection number
Ezekiel 37:27	Reading	55
Matthew 7:8; Luke 11:10	Reading	63
Matthew 16:13-19	Reading	65
Luke 19:1-10	Reading	74
John 2:13-22	Reading	75
John 4:19-24	Reading	76
Luke 19:9	The Litany of Supplication	74
John 4:19-24	The Litany of Supplication	76
Ephesians 4:2	The Litany of Supplication	102
1 Peter 2:4-5	The Litany of Supplication	111
Revelation 6:9	The Deposition of the Relics	115
Psalm 15	The Deposition of the Relics	15
1 Kings 8:22-23, 27-30	Prayer of Dedication	7
Matthew 5:14	Prayer of Dedication	61
John 15:5	Prayer of Dedication	84
Romans 6:3-7, 11	Prayer of Dedication	90
Ephesians 2:19-22	Prayer of Dedication	100
Hebrews 12:22	Prayer of Dedication	108
1 Peter 2:4-5	Prayer of Dedication	111
Revelation 21:2-3	Prayer of Dedication	117
Revelation 21:23-24	Prayer of Dedication	119
Genesis 28:11-18	The Anointing of the Altar	3

Biblical passage	Ceremony	Reflection number
Psalm 84	The Anointing of the Altar	30
1 Corinthians 3:9c	The Anointing of the Altar	92
Revelation 21:3	The Anointing of the Altar	117
Revelation 21:12-14	The Anointing of the Altar	118
2 Corinthians 2:14-15	The Incensation of the Altar and the Church	98
Revelation 8:3-4	The Incensation of the Altar and the Church	116
Psalm 138	The Incensation of the Altar and the Church	43
Psalm 141:2	The Incensation of the Altar and the Church	44
Romans 12:1	The Incensation of the Altar and the Church	91
Tobit 13:10, 13-14ab, 14c-15, 17	The Lighting of the Altar and the Church	12
Isaiah 60:1, 3	The Lighting of the Altar and the Church	51
Luke 2:32	The Lighting of the Altar and the Church	72
1 Chronicles 29:17-18	Offertory Antiphon	8
John 2:13-22	Preface	75
1 Corinthians 15:28	Preface	97
Ephesians 2:19-22	Preface	100
Ephesians 3:4	Preface	101
Colossians 2:9	Preface	105

Biblical passage	Ceremony	Reflection number
Colossians 3:14	Preface	106
1 Peter 2:4-5	Preface	111
Revelation 21:2	Preface	117
Revelation 21:14	Preface	118
Psalm 128	Communion	41
Isaiah 56:7 (Matthew 21:13; Mark 11:17; Luke 19:46)	Communion	49
Matthew 7:8; Luke 11:10	Communion	63
Psalm 147:12-20	The Inauguration of the Chapel of the Most Blessed Sacrament	45
Psalm 138:1-2	Prayer after Communion	43
Matthew 18:10	Prayer after Communion	66
John 11:51-52	The Blessing and Dismissal	82
1 Corinthians 3:16	The Blessing and Dismissal	92
Isaiah 56:7 (Matthew 21:13; Mark 11:17; Luke 19:46)	The Blessing and Dismissal	49

The Order of the Dedication of a Church in Which Sacred Celebrations Are Already Regularly Taking Place

Sometimes a new church is put to use before its dedication. Although the practice is not ideal, it happens. When the bishop finally arrives for the dedication, he leads appropriate ceremonies.

This ritual acknowledges that the building has already served sacred purposes by gathering the faithful for religious celebrations. It repeats much of the information from the previous chapter but makes a few adjustments. It omits the solemn opening of the doors. The ceremony of handing the church over to the bishop may be omitted or adapted. The rite of sprinkling the walls is omitted because the previous sacred celebrations inside have already purified the building. The ceremonies associated with the first proclamation of Scripture are omitted because the Word of God is already being proclaimed there.

Part One: The Introductory Rites

The people gather inside, and the clergy process to the sanctuary. All may sing Psalm 122 with the refrain, "God is in his holy place." This passage from Psalm 68 appropriately attests that the building in which it is now sung has already been made holy. Or all may sing, "Let us go rejoicing to the house of the Lord," from the pilgrimage psalm of joyful approach to the Jerusalem temple.

The bishop greets the people. If it seems appropriate, he may receive documents detailing the construction of the building and an explanation of the design of the church. He does not hand the key to the priest in charge as he does when presiding for the dedication at the first use of the new building.

The bishop blesses and sprinkles water on the people as a sign of their repentance, but also to help them recall their baptism. If the altar is completely new, he sprinkles it as well. All may sing an antiphon such as one from Ezekiel: "I saw water flowing from the Temple." The bishop concludes by asking God to "cleanse us who are the temple where he dwells."

All sing the Gloria, as they do on other festive occasions, and the bishop offers the collect. This prayer is the same one from Chapter II, which asks God to "pour out your grace upon this place" and upon "all who call upon you," so that God's Word and sacraments may strengthen the faithful who worship in this place.

Part Two: The Liturgy of the Word

All are seated for the readings from sacred Scripture. These take place in the usual way, except that no servers are to carry incense or candles as the gospel is proclaimed. Those symbols have an important part later in the ceremony.

The readings are specially chosen for this celebration. Those who prepare the liturgy may choose from a wide variety of passages from the Old Testament, its psalms, the New Testament, and its gospels.

The bishop preaches about the readings and the meaning of the celebration. All recite the Creed together, declaring the faith that binds the community celebrating the Eucharist here. The universal prayer is omitted because the Litany of the Saints will replace it.

Part Three: The Prayer of Dedication and the Anointings

The third part of the ceremony is a highlight of this gathering: the dedication of the church and the altar. It repeats all the material from the third part of Chapter II. For a more detailed commentary, see the treatment above.

All join in the litany of supplication, invoking the saints for their aid. If relics are to be embedded beneath the altar, these are brought forward. The bishop offers the solemn prayer of dedication and leads the anointing of the altar and the walls. The church is incensed, and its candles are set ablaze.

Part Four: The Liturgy of the Eucharist

As in Chapter II, the rest of the Mass of dedication is quite familiar to most Catholics. There are a few differences, however.

The preface for this liturgy was newly composed after the Second Vatican Council to account for the dedication of a building in which sacred celebrations are already taking place. It embraces several themes of the council, including the image of the pilgrim church on its journey toward the heavenly Jerusalem. A priest will proclaim this same preface each year on the anniversary of the church's dedication.

If the building has a new Blessed Sacrament chapel, the bishop may inaugurate it by bringing the ciborium of hosts there at the end of the distribution of communion. In most cases, however, if the building has been in use, so has its tabernacle, and this ceremony is omitted.

If your community is celebrating the dedication of a church already in use, you will hear many of the scriptural passages and biblical allusions from the dedication of a new church treated in Chapter II. Try to learn which of the many possible readings are proclaimed for the Liturgy of the Word. These biblical passages should assist your prayerful reflection:

Biblical passage	Ceremony	Reflection number
Genesis 28:11-18	Entrance	3
Psalm 68:6-7, 36	Entrance	29
Psalm 122	Entrance	39
Ezekiel 36:22-26	The Blessing and Sprinkling of Water	54
Ezekiel 47:1, 9	The Blessing and Sprinkling of Water	57
Romans 6:3-7	The Blessing and Sprinkling of Water	90
1 Corinthians 3:16	The Blessing and Sprinkling of Water	92
1 Corinthians 6:19	The Blessing and Sprinkling of Water	93
Hebrews 12:22	The Blessing and Sprinkling of Water	108
Revelation 21:2	The Blessing and Sprinkling of Water	117
1 Kings 8:22-23, 27-30	Reading	7

Biblical passage	Ceremony	Reflection number
2 Chronicles 5:6-10, 13–6:2	Reading	9
Isaiah 56:1, 6-7	Reading	49
Ezekiel 43:1-2, 4-7a	Reading	56
Ezekiel 47:1-2, 8-9, 12	Reading	57
Acts 7:44-50	Reading	88
Revelation 21:1-5a	Reading	117
Revelation 21:9b-14	Reading	118
1 Chronicles 29:10-13	Reading	8
Psalm 46:2-3, 5-6, 8-9	Reading	25
Psalm 84:3, 4, 5 and 10, 11	Reading	30
Psalm 95:1-2, 3-5, 6-7	Reading	32
Psalm 122:1-2, 3-4, 8-9	Reading	39
1 Corinthians 3:9c-11, 16-17	Reading	92
Ephesians 2:19-22	Reading	100
Hebrews 12:18-19, 22-24	Reading	108
1 Peter 2:4-5	Reading	111
2 Chronicles 7:16	Reading	10
Isaiah 66:1	Reading	52
Ezekiel 37:27	Reading	55

Biblical passage	Ceremony	Reflection number
Matthew 7:8; Luke 11:10	Reading	63
Matthew 16:13-19	Reading	65
Luke 19:1-10	Reading	74
John 2:13-22	Reading	75
John 4:19-24	Reading	76
Luke 19:9	The Litany of Supplication	74
John 4:19-24	The Litany of Supplication	76
Ephesians 4:2	The Litany of Supplication	102
1 Peter 2:4-5	The Litany of Supplication	111
Revelation 6:9	The Deposition of the Relics	115
Psalm 15	The Deposition of the Relics	15
1 Kings 8:22-23, 27-30	Prayer of Dedication	7
Matthew 5:14	Prayer of Dedication	61
John 15:5	Prayer of Dedication	84
Romans 6:3-7, 11	Prayer of Dedication	90
Ephesians 2:19-22	Prayer of Dedication	100
Hebrews 12:22	Prayer of Dedication	108
1 Peter 2:4-5	Prayer of Dedication	111
Revelation 21:2, 3	Prayer of Dedication	117
Revelation 21:23-24	Prayer of Dedication	119

Biblical passage	Ceremony	Reflection number
Genesis 28:11-18	The Anointing of the Altar	3
Psalm 84	The Anointing of the Altar	30
1 Corinthians 3:9c	The Anointing of the Altar	92
Revelation 21:3	The Anointing of the Altar	117
Revelation 21:12-14	The Anointing of the Altar	118
2 Corinthians 2:14-15	The Incensation of the Altar and the Church	98
Revelation 8:3-4	The Incensation of the Altar and the Church	116
Psalm 138	The Incensation of the Altar and the Church	43
Psalm 141:2	The Incensation of the Altar and the Church	44
Romans 12:1	The Incensation of the Altar and the Church	91
Tobit 13:10, 13-14ab, 14c-15, 17	The Lighting of the Altar and the Church	12
Isaiah 60:1, 3	The Lighting of the Altar and the Church	51
Luke 2:32	The Lighting of the Altar and the Church	72
1 Chronicles 29:17-18	Offertory Antiphon	8
1 Corinthians 3:16-17	Preface	92
1 Corinthians 6:19	Preface	93
2 Corinthians 6:16	Preface	99

Biblical passage	Ceremony	Reflection number
Ephesians 4:15-16	Preface	103
Hebrews 12:22	Preface	108
Revelation 3:12	Preface	113
Revelation 21:2-3	Preface	117
Psalm 147:12-20	The Inauguration of the Chapel of the Most Blessed Sacrament	45
Psalm 128	Communion	41
Isaiah 56:7 (Matthew 21:13; Mark 11:17; Luke 19:46)	Communion	49
Matthew 7:8; Luke 11:10	Communion	63
Psalm 138:1-2	Prayer after Communion	43
Matthew 18:10	Prayer after Communion	66
John 11:51-52	The Blessing and Dismissal	82
1 Corinthians 3:16	The Blessing and Dismissal	92
Isaiah 56:7 (Matthew 21:13; Mark 11:17; Luke 19:46)	The Blessing and Dismissal	49

CHAPTER IV

The Order of the Dedication of an Altar

Sometimes a previously dedicated church receives a new altar. The old altar may have proven inadequate due to its size, material, deterioration, or some other concern. The dedication takes place within Mass, using several of the elements from the previous chapters pertaining to the dedication of a church.

Part One: The Introductory Rites

The Mass begins as usual. For the entrance procession, the people may sing an antiphon and psalm, such as "Turn your eyes, O God, our shield, and look on the face of your Anointed one" from Psalm 84 or "I will come to the altar of God" from Psalm 43, which is also recommended for the verses.

When the bishop enters the sanctuary, he does not kiss the altar because it has not yet been dedicated. He greets the people, and he offers a blessing over the water to be sprinkled on them as a sign of their repentance and a renewal of their baptism. The bishop does not sprinkle the walls because the building has already been dedicated. He does sprinkle the altar to purify it in preparation for its dedication. The people may sing an antiphon, such as one from Ezekiel, "I saw water flowing from the Temple."

All sing the Gloria, as they commonly do on festive occasions, and the bishop offers the collect, a prayer special to this occasion. This collect was newly composed after the Second Vatican Council just for this purpose, to ask God "to fill [the] Church. . . with heavenly grace as she dedicates. . . this altar." The bishop thus prays at this moment not for the new altar, but for the people who will use it.

Part Two: The Liturgy of the Word

All are seated to listen to readings from Sacred Scripture. Special readings may be used, as long as the liturgical day does not demand its own. For example, if the altar is being dedicated on a Sunday of Advent, Lent, or Easter, then the readings previously assigned to that day remain in place.

Otherwise, those preparing the liturgy may choose from a broad selection of options from the Bible's rich library of passages pertaining to altars, and to the Christian interpretation of altars as symbols of Jesus Christ.

Part Three: The Prayer of Dedication and the Anointings

The center of this part of the celebration is the bishop's prayer of dedication. Much of this ceremony appears in the previous chapters on the dedication of a church because a church dedication includes an altar dedication. In this case, though, the elements pertaining to the church alone are omitted, such as the incensing of the walls and the lighting of candles on the walls.

The Litany of Supplication

Many Catholics are more familiar with the expression "Litany of the Saints" than with "litany of supplication." The two are essentially the same. The purpose of this classic chant is not simply to list the names of saints, but to invoke their aid for some intention. Even in the ceremonies of ordination of deacons, priests, and bishops, the litany is properly called "of supplication" because the church both on earth and in heaven is making supplication to God for some specific reason. In this case, the reason is the dedication of the altar. That intention is specifically mentioned near the end of the litany, when those leading it ask God to "Consecrate this altar for your worship."

The Deposition of the Relics
Relics are no longer required for the dedication of an altar. Therefore, this part of the ceremony may be omitted.

If the relics of a saint are to be set beneath the altar, these are brought forward. Representatives of the community may also present a document detailing the date of dedication, the name of the bishop, the title of the church, and the name of the saint whose relics are present. This document may be set beneath the altar together with the relics as the people sing, the bishop prays, and a stonemason seals the opening shut. See Chapter II above for more commentary.

The Prayer of Dedication
The bishop offers the prayer that anchors the center of this ceremony. Relying on prototypes from altar dedications of the past, this prayer glorifies the Lord, who was praised at the altars of Noah, Abraham, and Moses. It highlights the paschal mystery of Christ. It asks the Lord, "pour forth from heaven your sanctifying power upon this altar, built in the house of the Church, that it may be an altar dedicated for all time by the sacrifice of Christ, and stand as the Lord's table where your people are refreshed by the divine banquet." It will be both altar of sacrifice and table of communion.

As the bishop lists the future purposes of the altar, one can hear the echo of many themes of the Second Vatican Council: the spirit of "joy," the taking of "new paths ahead," "peace," the coming of "the Spirit," "the Church's unity," "praise and thanksgiving," and the hopes of this community to come "jubilant to eternal dwellings."

The Anointing of the Altar

The bishop puts on a special apron called a gremial to protect his other vestments as he anoints the altar. He takes in hand a vessel containing sacred chrism, the fragrant oil used at sacraments received only once in a lifetime: baptism, confirmation, and priestly ordination. The bishop prays that "this altar. . . may express the mystery of Christ, who offered himself to the Father for the life of the world."

All may sing an antiphon and psalm, such as "God, your God, has anointed you," with Psalm 45. Psalm 118 is recommended for Easter Time because it foreshadows Christ as the stone the builders rejected, who has become the cornerstone.

The Incensation of the Altar

The bishop ignites incense placed on top of the altar. Taking a thurible, he incenses the altar. Then a minister takes the thurible to incense the bishop and the people.

All may sing an antiphon and psalm, such as "An Angel stood by the altar of the Temple holding in his hand a golden censer," from the book of Revelation, along with Psalm 138, which praises God in the holy temple in the presence of angels.

The Covering and the Lighting of the Altar

Ministers may cover the altar with a cloth, decorate the area around the altar with flowers, and set candles and a cross on or near the altar. All these actions provide visual beauty to the newly dedicated altar.

The bishop lights the altar candles. Someone may turn on the electrical lights above the altar. The bishop prays that those who share in the Lord's Supper may "shine with his light." Those who will receive communion at this altar carry the light of the Gospel of Christ to the world.

Part Four: The Liturgy of the Eucharist

As the gifts are brought forward for the Eucharist, all may sing an antiphon such as the words of Jesus, "If you offer your gift at the altar, and there recall that your brother has something against you, leave your gift before the altar, go first and be reconciled." Another suggestion is that all sing of the altar that Moses consecrated, "sacrificing victims and offering holocausts upon it."

When the bishop approaches the newly dedicated altar, he kisses it. The celebrant usually performs this action at the beginning of a Mass, but in this case, he waits until after the dedication. He does not incense the altar at this time because he has just done so.

The bishop concludes the preparation of the gifts with a prayer that has been part of altar dedications since the eighth century. He invokes the Holy Spirit to come upon the altar "to sanctify the gifts" and "cleanse the hearts of all who receive them."

The preface was newly composed for this ritual after the Second Vatican Council, so in back-to-back prayers, the community hears one that is quite ancient and another that is quite new. This one resembles an older preface at the dedication of a church.

The preface honors Christ as the "true Priest and the true oblation." It declares that the altar will be "the table of the Lord," recalling a popular image from Psalm 23, where the people will be "fed by the Body of Christ" and drink "from the streams that flow from Christ, the spiritual rock."

At communion, the liturgy recommends Psalm 128, which celebrates the joy of families gathered around a table at home and applies the image to the parish family at the communion table.

The prayer after communion poetically and boldly asks that those who are nourished by Christ may be transformed into Christ. This entire celebration accomplishes more than the blessing of a piece of furniture. It prepares the table of communion for the Body of Christ in union with its head.

The bishop and deacon bless and dismiss the people as usual. The bishop's solemn blessing prays that all may exercise their baptismal priesthood, become one heart and one soul, and draw others to Christ when they proclaim their faith in him.

To reflect better on this richly symbolic ceremony, try to learn which of the many possible readings are proclaimed in the Liturgy of the Word. Additionally, these Scripture passages will guide your prayer:

Biblical passage	Ceremony	Reflection number
Psalm 42–43	Entrance	23
Psalm 84:10-11, 2-3	Entrance	30
Isaiah 56:1, 6-7 (Matthew 21:13; Mark 11:17; Luke 19:46); 59:21	Entrance	49
Ezekiel 36:22-26	The Blessing and Sprinkling of Water	54
Ezekiel 47:1, 9	The Blessing and Sprinkling of Water	57
Romans 6:3-7, 11	The Blessing and Sprinkling of Water	90

Biblical passage	Ceremony	Reflection number
1 Corinthians 3:16	The Blessing and Sprinkling of Water	92
1 Corinthians 6:19	The Blessing and Sprinkling of Water	93
Hebrews 12:22	The Blessing and Sprinkling of Water	108
Revelation 21:2	The Blessing and Sprinkling of Water	117
John 12:32	Collect	83
Genesis 28:11-18	Reading	3
Joshua 8:30-35	Reading	5
1 Maccabees 4:52-59	Reading	13
Acts 2:42-47	Reading	86
Revelation 8:3-4	Reading	116
Revelation 21:3b	Reading	117
Psalm 84:3, 4, 5, and 10, 11	Reading	30
Psalm 95:1-2, 3-5, 6-7	Reading	32
Psalm 118:15-16, 19-20, 22-23, 27	Reading	37
Psalm 119:105a, 129, 130, 133, 135, 144	Reading	38
Psalm 122:1-2, 3-4, 8-9	Reading	39
1 Corinthians 10:16-21	Reading	95
Hebrews 13:8-15	Reading	109

Biblical passage	Ceremony	Reflection number
Ezekiel 37:27	Reading	55
Matthew 5:23-24	Reading	62
John 4:19-24	Reading	76
John 12:31-36a	Reading	83
Revelation 6:9	The Deposition of the Relics	115
Psalm 15	The Deposition of the Relics	15
Genesis 8:20-21	The Prayer of Dedication	1
Genesis 22:9-10	The Prayer of Dedication	2
Exodus 24:4-6	The Prayer of Dedication	4
John 19:34	The Prayer of Dedication	85
Romans 4:9-11	The Prayer of Dedication	89
Revelation 5:6	The Prayer of Dedication	114
Genesis 28:11-18	The Anointing of the Altar	3
Hebrews 1:9	The Anointing of the Altar	22
Psalm 45 (Hebrews 1:9)	The Anointing of the Altar	24
Psalm 118	The Anointing of the Altar	37
2 Corinthians 2:14-15	The Incensation of the Altar and the Church	98
Revelation 8:3-4	The Incensation of the Altar and the Church	116
Psalm 138	The Incensation of the Altar and the Church	43

Biblical passage	Ceremony	Reflection number
Psalm 141:2	The Incensation of the Altar and the Church	44
Psalm 36:10	The Lighting of the Altar	22
Luke 2:32	The Lighting of the Altar	72
Exodus 24:4-6	Offertory Antiphon	4
Matthew 5:23-24	Offertory Antiphon	62
Psalm 23:1-3a, 3b-4, 5-6	Preface	18
Psalm 110:4	Preface	35
Isaiah 12:3	Preface	46
Jeremiah 30:18	Preface	53
Malachi 1:11	Preface	60
John 6:54-55	Preface	78
John 7:37-39	Preface	81
John 11:51-52	Preface	82
1 Corinthians 10:1-6	Preface	94
1 Corinthians 11:23-28	Preface	96
Ephesians 5:2	Preface	104
Hebrews 4:14; 5:5-6	Preface	107
1 Peter 2:4-5	Preface	111
Psalm 84:2-5, 9-11	Communion	30
Psalm 128	Communion	41

CHAPTER V

The Order of Blessing a Church

For the blessing of a church that serves as a chapel or oratory, the bishop conducts a simpler ceremony, though one still filled with meaning. The building will not be used in all the ways of a parish church, but it will still serve as an important place for prayer.

Part One: The Introductory Rites

The community gathers as usual before the entrance procession. Because the bishop will later bless the altar, he does not kiss nor incense it as he enters the sanctuary. He greets the people and blesses water to be sprinkled on them as a sign of repentance and a remembrance of their baptism. He will also sprinkle the walls for their purification. The bishop reminds the people that, together with him, all of them "make up the living Church, placed in the world as a sign and witness of the love" of God.

All may sing the Gloria, as they do on festive occasions. The bishop invites all to pray before he leads the collect. If the blessing takes place on an important day of the liturgical calendar, he offers the prayer assigned to that day. Otherwise, he prays a special collect, asking God for a blessing "on this church, which you have permitted us to build" and asks that all who assemble in it "may know the presence of Jesus Christ."

Part Two: The Liturgy of the Word

The readings take place in the usual way. At the gospel, however, ministers do not carry incense or candles because these will be introduced later in the ceremony. All recite the Creed and the universal prayer.

The blessing will not begin with the Litany of the Saints as the dedications of a church and altar do. In some cases, however, the altar is being dedicated, and that would call for the litany instead of the universal prayer.

Part Three: The Blessing of the Altar

All may sing an antiphon such as one based on Psalm 128: "Like shoots of the olive, may the children of the Church be gathered around the table of the Lord." These words apply the ancient psalm to the contemporary gathering of the Christian family around the communion table.

The bishop invites all to a period of silent prayer before he offers the blessing. The prayer borrows many ideas from the preface for the Mass of the dedication of an altar, as described above in Chapter II. It prays that the altar may be "the center of . . . praise and thanksgiving," where the "bread of life" is broken and believers "drink of the cup of unity." All answer, "Blessed be God for ever."

The bishop does not anoint this altar with chrism, making a distinction between this blessed altar and the one that is dedicated in a parish church as in the previous chapters.

Part Four: The Liturgy of the Eucharist

The altar is covered with a cloth. Flowers are brought forward to decorate the area around it. All many sing an antiphon, such as "If you offer your gifts" or "Moses consecrated an altar," recalling biblical passages from both testaments about the proper usage of a sacred table. The bishop may incense the altar. These ceremonies resemble those that follow the anointing of an altar in a dedicated church, as described in the previous chapters.

As the gifts are brought forward, the bishop kisses the altar for the first time, now that it has been blessed. After setting the gifts on the corporal, he does not incense the altar again.

The liturgy continues as usual through the sharing of communion. If there is a Blessed Sacrament chapel, the bishop may inaugurate it as in the dedication of a church. Afterward, he and the deacon conclude the ceremony with the blessing and dismissal.

This simple ceremony of blessing honors the new space for worship. Those wishing to reflect on its meaning may find these biblical passages inspiring:

Biblical passage	Ceremony	Reflection number
Ezekiel 36:22-26	The Blessing and Sprinkling of Water	54
Matthew 18:20	Collect	67
Isaiah 12:3	The Blessing of the Altar	46
John 6:35, 48	The Blessing of the Altar	77
John 7:37-39	The Blessing of the Altar	81
Romans 12:1	The Blessing of the Altar	91

Biblical passage	Ceremony	Reflection number
1 Peter 2:4-5	The Blessing of the Altar	111
Exodus 24:4-6	Offertory Antiphon	4
Matthew 5:23-24	Offertory Antiphon	62
John 11:51-52	The Blessing and Dismissal	82
1 Corinthians 3:16	The Blessing and Dismissal	92
Isaiah 56:7 (Matthew 21:13; Mark 11:17; Luke 19:46)	The Blessing and Dismissal	49

CHAPTER VI

The Order of Blessing an Altar

This ceremony applies to a movable altar that may be used for the celebration of Mass. The altar may be located in a multipurpose space or even brought to a designated place for Mass as needed. This altar is "blessed," not "dedicated," and the no relics of saints may therefore be placed beneath it. The church has a long history of blessing such altars because of the desire to celebrate Mass occasionally outside a dedicated church.

The bishop or a priest may bless this altar at any Mass, using the prayers and readings assigned to the liturgical day. The introductory rites and the Liturgy of the Word, then, take place as usual.

After the universal prayer, the presider goes to the altar while all sing an antiphon, such as "Like shoots of the olive." This passage applies an image from Psalm 128 to this ceremony, a church family gathered around the table of its altar for a sacred meal. The presider invites the people to join silently in prayer. He uses the prayer found in Chapter V, the Order of Blessing a Church, because that ceremony includes a separate blessing of the altar.

The presider sprinkles the altar with blessed water and incenses it. A minister incenses the presider and the people. The altar is covered with a cloth, and the area is decorated with flowers, candles, and a cross. All may sing an antiphon, such as "If you offer your gift" from the blessing of a church. The presider kisses the altar for the first time, and the preparation of the gifts takes place as usual, though without an additional incensation of the altar.

Mass continues in the usual way through the Liturgy of the Eucharist and the final blessing and dismissal. This simple liturgy is nonetheless quite lovely and meaningful. It designates a special furnishing for the celebration of the Mass. To reflect on this ceremony, you may find these readings helpful:

Biblical passage	Ceremony	Reflection number
Isaiah 12:3	The Blessing of the Altar	46
John 6:35, 48	The Blessing of the Altar	77
John 7:37-39	The Blessing of the Altar	81
Romans 12:1	The Blessing of the Altar	91
1 Peter 2:4-5	The Blessing of the Altar	111
Matthew 5:23-24	Offertory Antiphon	62

CHAPTER VII

The Order of Blessing a Chalice and a Paten

Any priest may bless a chalice and a paten, but in the past this ceremony belonged to a bishop. Because of that tradition, it appears within the volume of *The Order of the Dedication of a Church and an Altar* in two versions—one during Mass and one apart from Mass. The ceremony during Mass can also be found in the Roman Missal, making it more accessible to any priest.

If the blessing takes place on a weekday in Ordinary Time, the liturgy may incorporate special readings. Otherwise, the readings of the day are proclaimed.

After the Liturgy of the Word, ministers or representatives of the community place the vessels to be blessed on the altar. All may sing an antiphon, such as "The chalice of salvation I will raise, and I will call on the name of the Lord."

At the altar, the priest offers a prayer. If this takes place during Mass, the priest does not actually bless the vessels. When their contents are consecrated as the Body and Blood of Christ, those elements thereby bless the vessels. The priest therefore prays, "may the Body and Blood of your Son, offered and received by means of these vessels, make them holy." Outside of Mass, when the vessels are not immediately put to use, the prayer of the priest does indeed bless them.

The priest also prays that the people be renewed by the sacraments and come with the saints to the banquet in the kingdom of heaven. He thus looks beyond the present celebration of the Mass toward the blessed future of eternal life.

After these prayers, if the ceremony takes place during Mass, ministers place the corporal on the altar, and some of the faithful bring forward the gifts for the celebration. Mass continues in the usual way. A modified version of the antiphon that opened the rite may be sung during the preparation of the gifts, especially because the chalice is being filled with its wine and water: "The chalice of salvation I will raise, and I will offer a sacrifice of praise." It is recommended that the priest incense the altar and the gifts, and that the faithful receive not only the Body of Christ at communion, but also the Blood of Christ, from the newly blessed chalice.

This simple ceremony profoundly sets aside special vessels for the most sacred moments of the Mass: the consecration of bread and wine into the Body and Blood of Christ and the sharing of Holy Communion. If you experience this ritual, you may want to learn beforehand which readings will be used. You will find helpful a reflection on these scriptural passages:

Biblical passage	Ceremony	Reflection number
Psalm 116:10-19	Entrance	36
1 Corinthians 10:14-22a	Reading	95
1 Corinthians 11:23-28	Reading	96
Psalm 16:5 and 8, 9-10, 11	Reading	16

Biblical passage	Ceremony	Reflection number
Psalm 23:1-3a, 3b-4, 5-6	Reading	18
John 6:56, 57	Reading	79
Matthew 20:20-28	Reading	68
Mark 14:12-16, 22-26	Reading	71
Psalm 116:13	Blessing	36
Psalm 116:10-19	Preparation of the Gifts	36
Psalm 116:13	Universal Prayer	36
Matthew 26:39	Universal Prayer	69
John 6:35, 48	Universal Prayer	77

CHAPTER VIII

The Anniversary of the Dedication of the Church

E ach year, the parish celebrates the anniversary of the dedication of its church with a solemnity. Even if it falls on a weekday, the liturgy resembles a Sunday: Two readings and a responsorial psalm precede the proclamation of the gospel. All sing the Gloria and recite the Creed. The Mass may conclude with a solemn blessing.

The Missal and the lectionary offer special prayers and readings for this occasion. The options are many, so you may want to obtain some information in advance. Most importantly, when is the anniversary of dedication of your parish church? How will it be celebrated this year? Which antiphons and readings will be used for the liturgy? You will find references to them in the table below:

Biblical passage	Ceremony	Reflection number
Genesis 28:17, 22	Entrance	3
Psalm 5	Entrance	14
Psalm 68: 6-7, 36	Entrance	29

Biblical passage	Ceremony	Reflection number
Psalm 84	Entrance	30
Isaiah 56:7	Entrance	49
Isaiah 59:21	Entrance	50
Malachi 1:11	Collect	60
Psalm 130:7	Collect	42
1 Kings 8:22-23, 27-30	Reading	7
2 Chronicles 5:6-10, 13–6:2	Reading	9
Isaiah 56:1, 6-7	Reading	49
Ezekiel 43:1-2, 4-7a	Reading	56
Ezekiel 47:1-2, 8-9, 12	Reading	57
Acts 7:44-50	Reading	88
1 Chronicles 29:10-13	Reading	8
Psalm 46:2-3, 5-6, 8-9	Reading	25
Psalm 84:3, 4, 5, and 10, 11	Reading	30
Psalm 95:1-2, 3-5, 6-7	Reading	32
Psalm 122:1-2, 3-4, 8-9	Reading	39
Genesis 28:16-17	Reading	3
1 Corinthians 3:9c-11, 16-17	Reading	92
Ephesians 2:19-22	Reading	100
Hebrews 12:18-19, 22-24	Reading	108

Biblical passage	Ceremony	Reflection number
1 Peter 2:4-5	Reading	111
Revelation 21:1-5a	Reading	117
Revelation 21:9b-14	Reading	118
2 Chronicles 7:16	Reading	10
Isaiah 66:1	Reading	52
Ezekiel 37:27	Reading	55
Revelation 21:3b	Reading	117
Matthew 7:8; Luke 11:10	Reading	63
Matthew 16:18	Reading	65
Psalm 138:2	Reading	43
Psalm 26:8	Reading	20
Psalm 122:1	Reading	39
Psalm 65:2	Reading	28
Psalm 125:1-2	Reading	40
Matthew 16:13-18	Reading	65
Luke 19:1-10	Reading	74
John 2:13-22	Reading	75
John 4:19-24	Reading	76
Exodus 24:4-6	Offertory	4
1 Chronicles 29:17-18	Offertory	8
Psalm 138	Offertory	43
Matthew 16:18	Offertory	65

Biblical passage	Ceremony	Reflection number
Daniel 9:4, 17, 19	Offertory	59
Exodus 24:4, 5	Offertory	4
Revelation 8:3, 4	Offertory	116
Ezekiel 43:1-2, 4-7a	Prayer over the Offerings	56
Romans 12:1	Prayer over the Offerings	91
1 Corinthians 3:16-17	Preface	92
1 Corinthians 6:19	Preface	93
2 Corinthians 6:16	Preface	99
Ephesians 4:15-16	Preface	103
Hebrews 12:22	Preface	108
Revelation 3:12	Preface	113
Revelation 21:2-3	Preface	117
1 Corinthians 3:16-17	Communion	92
Isaiah 56:7 (Matthew 21:13; Mark 11:17; Luke 19:46)	Communion	49
Matthew 7:8; Luke 11:10	Communion	63
Psalm 84:2-5, 9-11	Communion	30
Psalm 51:21	Communion	27
Psalm 122:3-4	Communion	39
Psalm 43:4	Communion	23
Psalm 96:8-9	Communion	33

Biblical passage	Ceremony	Reflection number
Psalm 27:4	Communion	21
Psalm 147:12-20	Communion	45
John 11:51-52	The Blessing	82
1 Corinthians 3:16	The Blessing	92
Isaiah 56:7 (Matthew 21:13; Mark 11:17; Luke 19:46)	The Blessing	49

THE
REFLECTIONS

Old Testament

1. Genesis 8:20-21

In the Bible

As the flood waters recede, Noah builds an altar to the Lord and sacrifices burnt offerings of animals. "When the Lord smelled the pleasing odor, the Lord said in his heart, 'I will never again curse the ground because of humankind.'"

In the Liturgy

When the bishop comes to dedicate an altar in a church that has already been dedicated (Chapter IV), he praises God for those who built altars in the past, including Noah, "a second father of the human race." God the Father accepted Noah's offering, renewing his "covenant of love with the human race."

In Your Heart

When you come to Mass and see the gifts brought to the altar, you may imitate in your heart what Moses did.

What "floodwaters" have receded for you in your life? How has God rescued you from danger?

What elements of new life do you see around you?

What sacrifice can you bring to the altar in your church? What can you offer God that will cause a pleasing aroma?

2. Genesis 22:9-10

In the Bible

Abraham takes his only son Isaac and prepares to sacrifice him at the Lord's command. He "built an altar there and laid the wood in order. He bound his son Isaac, and laid him on the altar, on top of the wood." Abraham unsheathes his knife, but an angel of the Lord stops him and praises him for fearing God.

In the Liturgy

When the bishop dedicates a new altar in a church that has already been dedicated (Chapter IV), he praises God for those who built altars in the past, including Abraham, "our father in faith." He "constructed an altar," ready to sacrifice his son, his dearest possession, in order to please God.

In Your Heart

Especially if you have children, you know the force of a parent's love and of your love for God. You would never harm your child. You love God's commands.

Who are the people you love the most, the ones you keep in your prayers?

What is the hardest thing that God has asked you to do?

What sacrifice is God asking of you right now? Bring that sacrifice to your church's new altar.

3. Genesis 28:11-18

In the Bible

On his way toward Haran, as the sun is setting, Jacob lies down on the ground and positions a rock for his pillow. In a dream he sees a ladder stretching from the earth to heaven, "and the angels of God were ascending and descending on it." God appears to Jacob and promises him land, many offspring, and perpetual accompaniment. Jacob says, "the Lord is in this place. . . . How awesome is this place! This is none other than the house of God, and this is the gate of heaven." Jacob takes the stone he had used that night, sets it up as a pillar, "and pour[s] oil on the top of it."

In the Liturgy

This is one of the readings that may be proclaimed at the dedication of a new altar in a church that has already been dedicated (Chapter IV). It inspired one of the entrance antiphons for the dedication of a new church, "God is in his holy place" (Chapters II and III), as well as the introit and the gradual that may replace the responsorial psalm for the anniversary of the dedication of the church (Chapter VIII).

When the bishop anoints a new altar, he performs an action similar to Jacob's (Chapters II, III, and IV).

In Your Heart

In your private prayer, you have experienced the presence of God and the promise of God. You have received some reassurances and formed strong memories.

In what place have you especially encountered God? Where have you been that seems to join earth to heaven so closely that a ladder could bring you from one place to the other?

What object in your possession is a symbol of God's promises to you?

Jacob consecrated a special object with oil. What have you done to set apart something special to you?

4. Exodus 24:4-6

In the Bible

After Moses wrote down the commandments of the Lord, he rose early the next morning "and built an altar at the foot of the mountain." He ordered the slaughtering of oxen in sacrifice, he sprinkled half the blood on the altar, and he put half in basins to be sprinkled on the people as a sign of their covenant with the Lord.

In the Liturgy

When the bishop dedicates a new altar in a church that has already been dedicated (Chapter IV), his prayer of dedication praises God for those who built altars in the past, including Moses, "the mediator of the old Law," who sprinkled blood on the altar mystically to "prefigure the altar of the Cross."

The people may sing part of this passage as the gifts are brought to the altar for the first time on three different occasions: after the dedication of a new altar in a previously dedicated church (Chapter IV), at the blessing of a church to be used as a chapel or oratory (Chapter V), or on the anniversary of the dedication of a church (Chapter VIII). The antiphon begins, "Moses consecrated an altar to the Lord, sacrificing victims and offering holocausts upon it."

In Your Heart

The altar in your local church stands in a long line of altars set aside for celebrating the sacrifice of the Mass. Even before Christ, Israel fulfilled its covenant with God by offering sacrifices on altars.

What is the daily altar of your sacrifice? What is the table, desk, bench, or counter where you expend your energy?

For whom do you sacrifice? What goals make your work worthwhile?

How do you consecrate your work to God?

5. Joshua 8:30-35

In the Bible

Joshua sets aside a natural stone as an altar to the Lord, one that no human implements have hewn. He offers sacrifices upon it, and then writes a copy of the law of Moses onto the altar stone. He then reads the entire book of the law of Moses to the gathered assembly.

In the Liturgy
The lectionary offers this as one option for the first reading at Mass when a new altar is dedicated inside a previously dedicated church (Chapter IV). As people prepare for the first sacrifice of the Mass upon the new altar, they hear how Joshua had set aside a new stone for offering sacrifice and as a place to proclaim God's Word to the people.

In Your Heart
Think about the new altar in your church. How will it be used? How is it decorated? Is there writing upon it? Do images adorn it?

Do you have raw stones anywhere in your home? What do they signify to you? Is it important that they are natural, that no one has carved them? Why?

Do you have a favorite biblical quote carved, imprinted, or handwritten somewhere in your home? What does it say? What does that passage mean to you?

6. 1 Kings 5:16-32 (2-18)

In the Bible
Solomon begins the construction of the temple in Jerusalem by ordering cedar logs from Lebanon and blocks of cut stone. The skilled Sidonians cut the timber and place the logs in sailboats for transport. Tens of thousands of additional workers cut rocks from the mountains and carry them to Jerusalem as the foundation for the temple.

The verses of chapter 5 from the First Book of Kings are not numbered the same in every biblical translation. You will find them either in 16-32 or 2-18.

In the Liturgy
This is one of the suggestions for the first reading in the Order of Laying a Foundation Stone or Commencement of Work on the Building of a Church (Chapter I). People hear it outdoors on the site where the new church will be built.

In Your Heart
Your new parish church requires a lot of building material. Where does it come from? Who brings it here?

In your personal life, how have you shared in a building project? Was it as large as a home or as small as a child's toy? How much of the beginning do you remember?

As your parish begins the construction of a new church, think about the laborers who will bring it into reality. How would you like to pray for them?

7. 1 Kings 8:22-23, 27-30

In the Bible
Solomon offers a solemn prayer of dedication for the newly built temple in Jerusalem. He stands before the altar and extends his arms to heaven. He wonders if God, who needs no temple, will indeed dwell here. He recalls God's promises and asks God to hear the prayers that will be offered forever in this holy place.

In the Liturgy
This is one option for the first reading on the anniversary of the dedication of your parish church (Chapter VIII). The readings may change from year to year.

Solomon's words also served as a model for the dedication prayer that the bishop offers for a new church (Chapter II). Although the bishop's prayer does not directly borrow images from this passage, it imitates the style.

The entire passage is one option for the first reading at the dedication of a church already in use (Chapter III). It places the building within the long history of sacred spaces set aside for worship.

In Your Heart

What postures do you use for prayer? Like Solomon, do you ever stand before the altar? Do you ever extend your arms toward heaven? When do you kneel to pray? When do you sit? What difference does your posture make?

If your parish has a newly dedicated church building, how are you praying to God about it? Have you envisioned you and your family there in the years to come? Doing what? What do you most want God to do for this church being dedicated?

If you are celebrating the anniversary of your parish church, what memories do these walls bring you? For which past events in that church do you most want to thank God?

8. 1 Chronicles 29:10-13, 17-18

In the Bible

At the end of his life, King David realizes that he will not live to see the construction of the temple he longed to build. That task would fall to his son Solomon. In his last recorded prayer before his death, David offers his material wealth to help his son realize the dream. David hopes that all the people will follow his example of offering their possessions to God freely, joyously, and with an upright heart.

In the Liturgy

The first verses from this passage may be sung as the responsorial at the dedication of a church already in use (Chapter III) or on the anniversary of the dedication (Chapter VIII). They praise God, who helped generations past and who still rules victorious over all.

The final verses are recommended as the antiphon during the preparation of the gifts at the dedication of a church (Chapters II and III). As the altar is being used for the first time, the people remember the selflessness of King David and offer their gifts and their upright hearts to God. These same verses are also recommended at the same moment during the Mass that celebrates the anniversary of a church's dedication (Chapter VIII).

In Your Heart

Can you trace the faith back through the generations in your family? How did your ancestors praise God?

Who are the people who made the greatest sacrifices for the construction of your parish church? Some of their names may be on windows or plaques. What do you know of them?

Other names may not be remembered at all, but they were probably essential to the construction. Pray for the benefactors who made it possible for you to worship here.

What do you hope your legacy will be? How will future generations want to imitate your upright heart?

9. 2 Chronicles 5:6-10, 13–6:2

In the Bible

King Solomon offers sacrifices before the ark of the covenant, and then priests carry the ark into the temple. The cherubim spread their wings over the ark, within which are the two tablets of the commandments that God gave to Moses. The glory of the Lord fills the house like a cloud. Solomon declares that this will be God's dwelling place forever.

In the Liturgy
This passage is one of the options for the first reading at the Mass of dedication of a church already in use (Chapter III) or on the anniversary of the dedication of the church (Chapter VIII). These readings may change from year to year.

In Your Heart
In some churches, the tabernacle is designed to resemble this description of the ark of the covenant. Images of angels spreading their wings may cover the top.

What does the tabernacle look like in your church? How does it resemble the ark of the covenant, the place where God's glory dwelled in the Jerusalem temple and which stored some of the manna from the Exodus?

As you celebrate the anniversary of your church, think back on significant moments there. When did you most experience the glory of God filling the temple of your parish church?

When have you experienced the glory of the Lord in a church building? What made that day special?

10. 2 Chronicles 7:1, 14, 16

In the Bible
When Solomon finishes his prayer to dedicate the temple in Jerusalem, fire comes down from heaven to consume the offerings. The Lord speaks to Solomon in the night, promising to hear the people's prayers if they turn from their wicked ways and revere, love, and follow him. The Lord says that he has indeed chosen this temple as his dwelling place forever. The Lord's eyes and heart will be there for all time.

In the Liturgy

When the construction of the new church gets underway, the ceremony held on the new site opens with a prayer that recalls God's request that the people revere, love, and follow him (Chapter I). If they do, the glory of the Lord that once filled Solomon's temple will also fill them.

If Psalm 24 is chosen as the responsorial for this ceremony (Chapter I), 2 Chronicles 7:16a becomes the refrain: "I have chosen and consecrated this place."

The same ceremony ends with concluding rites that refer twice to the people as the temple of God's glory (Chapter I). As God chose to dwell in the Jerusalem temple of old, so God will dwell in this parish church, but also in the people who worship there.

For the dedication Mass (Chapters II and III) and for anniversary Mass of the dedication of the church (Chapter VIII), one of the possible verses for the gospel acclamation comes from this passage: "I have chosen and consecrated this place." It recalls how God chose Solomon's temple of old and how God chose this parish church as the place where he dwells.

In Your Heart

God promised to hear the prayers of people who revere him, love him, and follow him. Can you give examples of your response to God in all three of these areas?

How do you revere God? Where are you when you sense that you are doing it?

How do you love God? Are there times of your day when this is especially easy? Or hard?

How do you follow God? What has God asked you to do? Have you ever said no? How have you said yes?

11. Nehemiah 8:1-4a, 5-6, 8-10

In the Bible

Having rediscovered the lost book of the Law of Moses, the people assemble to hear Ezra the priest read it. Carpenters make a special wooden platform. Ezra stands on it, above the people, opens the scroll, and reads it. The people lift up their hands and answer, "Amen, Amen." They bow their heads to the ground and worship God.

In the Liturgy

This reading is required at the dedication of every newly built church, even in Easter Time when the first reading otherwise comes from the New Testament (Chapter II). The people of the parish imitate the people of old: After they gather together, a reader steps up to an elevated place, opens the book of the Scripture, and reads. The people worship God and make an acclamation at the conclusion of the proclamation. This reading is always the first one proclaimed from the new ambo of the church being dedicated.

In Your Heart

Where is the ambo in your parish church? Where do you sit in relationship to it? How do you stay attentive to the readings when they are proclaimed at Mass?

Have you rediscovered the Bible in your life? How did that happen? Is it more a part of your prayer today than it was in the past?

Where do you keep a Bible at home? How do you use it?

12. Tobit 13:10, 13-14ab, 14c-15, 17 (Clementine Vulgate)

In the Bible
Tobit's son Tobiah has returned from his journey with a new friend, the angel Raphael; a new wife, Sarah; and a new cure for Tobit's blindness, fish gall. The happy ending to his son's travels prompts Tobit to compose and sing a hymn of praise to God, whose holy city, Jerusalem, will shine with splendid light.

The words of this chapter are not the same in every translation. These particular verses may be difficult to find, but the spirit of the whole chapter remains the same.

In the Liturgy
After the bishop dedicates a new church and anoints its altar and walls, candles are lighted in celebration (Chapters II and III). These candles signify the light of the Gospel shining from this church for all to see, as well as the place for the celebration of the Eucharist. As ministers light the candles, all may sing a hymn of praise. The Canticle of Tobit is suggested for its declaration that God's holy city, Jerusalem, will shine with light. The light is not merely for the convenience of worshipers, but to guide all the nations toward Christ.

In Your Heart
When do you light candles at home? Do they create an atmosphere of warmth and care? Or do they signal hope in times of distress?

How does the exterior of your church serve as a symbol of Christ? What do passersby experience when they see the building? What do they learn of Christ?

Does your home shine the light of Christ? How do people recognize Christ by the light that comes from your home?

How do you praise God when you receive the answer to a prayer?

13. 1 Maccabees 4:52-59

In the Bible

After recovering the captured temple and restoring its profaned beauty, Judas Maccabaeus and his men offer sacrifice on the new altar for the first time. They dedicate the new altar with music, bow their faces to the ground, offer sacrifice for eight days, and decorate the front. They agree to observe the dedication on this date every year.

In the Liturgy

This is one of the readings suggested for Mass at the dedication of an altar in a church that has already been dedicated (Chapter IV). Especially if the previous altar had deteriorated or could no longer adequately serve its purpose, this reading poses some parallels for the community today. The site has already been held in honor. Now a new altar restores beauty at the church's center.

In Your Heart

Your church's new altar replaces a previous one. What do you recall of the former altar? What happened to it? How does the new altar better serve the community?

How have you experienced the loss and restoration of something dear in your life? What important possession was stolen, destroyed, or suffered deterioration? How did you address your grief?

What has replaced that loss? How does the new object compare with the previous one?

What differences did these events cause for you? Are you more tolerant of loss? Are you more grateful for God's everlasting providence?

14. Psalm 5

In the Bible

A solitary worshiper asks God for an answer to prayer. This person sings, "I enter your house. I bow down before your holy temple, in awe of you." The petitions are for the person's own justice and the declaration of the enemy's guilt. The psalmist reminds God that those who rejoice are those who love his name. The psalmist will be one of them when God grants this prayer.

In the Liturgy

Verses of this psalm may follow the entrance antiphon at the annual celebration of the parish church's dedication (Chapter VIII). The people enter God's house and bow down before their Lord, in awe of his power. They pray for their own justice and the right judgment of evildoers. If the relics of a saint are sealed beneath the altar, the people remember that the saints who loved God's name rejoice with him eternally.

In Your Heart

As you enter your parish church on the anniversary of its dedication, what petitions do you bring? Do you sense awe in the presence of God's holy house?

How are you asking God to make you a better lover of justice? As you acknowledge your sins, how could God make you a better person?

Who are those afflicting you? What evil acts cause you worry? Place these concerns into the hands of God, who dwells in the sacred space you call your parish church.

15. Psalm 15

In the Bible

The psalm asks God who may dwell in his holy place. It answers the question with the virtues that a person should possess: Those who do what is upright and who speak the truth, those who do no wrong and keep their promises. It reminds those who want to enter the Jerusalem temple that they should be as beautiful inside as the building where God dwells.

In the Liturgy
This psalm is recommended for the placement of the relics of a saint beneath a new altar (Chapters II, III, and IV). The Catholic Church no longer requires placing relics beneath altars, but the custom continues where it is desirable and where the relics can be verified.

As the bishop places the relics in the opening prepared for them, the community may sing Psalm 15. As the psalm declares that those who live an upright life are worthy to dwell in God's holy place, the relics of saints who dwell in heaven come to rest inside this newly dedicated altar.

In Your Heart
Does your parish church have the relics of saints beneath its altar? Who are they? What do you know of their lives?

Who are the saints who have inspired you? Whom do you claim as a patron saint? Why?

In your own family and circle of friends, are there people you consider to be saints? What virtues do they possess?

As you pray Psalm 15, what virtuous people come to mind? How must you change to become more like them?

16. Psalm 16:5 and 8, 9-10, 11

In the Bible
This psalm prays for protection, especially during the night. It places complete trust in God and pledges to avoid false worship. The singer calls the Lord "my portion and my cup." God

will not abandon his holy ones in death but will show them the path to life.

In the Liturgy

When a priest blesses a new chalice and paten during Mass, this psalm may be sung as the responsorial (Chapter VII). It makes an explicit reference to a cup.

The chalice of the Mass will hold the Blood of Christ, the Son of God, the holy one whom the Father raised from death to new life. The chalice at the Mass signifies our complete trust in God who loves us and redeems us. The Lord alone is our portion and our cup.

In Your Heart

What thoughts come to your mind during the consecration of the Mass? How does it stir your faith and trust in God?

How have you made the Lord your portion and your cup? How do you choose Christ above all other desires?

Do you have a favorite cup at home? What does it symbolize for you? Why?

17. Psalm 19:8-9, 10, 15

In the Bible

Psalm 19 divides into two parts, the first praising God for creation and the second praising God for the law. The themes interrelate, as God has stitched the outlines of good law into the goodness of the created cosmos. The particular verses here praise the wisdom we receive from God's law and the desire that our words will be as pleasing to God as his words are to us.

In the Liturgy

These verses serve as the responsorial psalm for the dedication of a new church (Chapter II). They are required at every such occasion, following the obligatory first reading from Nehemiah about the public proclamation of the rediscovered law of God. As the first psalm to be sung from the new ambo in a new church, it praises the Word of the Lord that will be proclaimed here.

In Your Heart

Many people instinctively love the beauty of creation but struggle to find the beauty in law. Still, listening to God's Word and acting on it bring order and peace to one's life.

What are two or three of your favorite Scripture passages? Why do these come to mind? How do they guide you?

When have you felt challenged by what you heard in the Bible or preached from the ambo?

Recall a time when you were later able to return to a challenging word and praise God for its beauty.

18. Psalm 23:1-3a, 3b-4, 5-6

In the Bible

The most beloved psalm of all, Psalm 23, introduces the enduring image of the Lord as shepherd. He guides the person praying this psalm along the right path, offering protection from evil in the valley of the shadow of death. The shepherd even provides a table where the follower may dine with an overflowing cup. The Lord shepherds his people for length of days unending.

In the Liturgy

At the dedication of a new altar in a previously dedicated church, the bishop uses a special preface to introduce the eucharistic prayer (Chapter IV). It borrows a number of images from the Bible, including one from Psalm 23. The bishop refers to the new altar when he says, "Here is prepared the table of the Lord." It recalls the joyful reflection in this psalm: "You have prepared a table before me."

The same psalm appears in the ceremony of the blessing of a chalice and paten (Chapter VII). During the Liturgy of the Word, it may serve as the responsorial. Again, it applies the verse about an overflowing cup at the Lord's table to the chalice that provides unending joy at the banquet of the Eucharist.

In Your Heart

Think of a satisfying meal you have recently eaten. What was the menu? What was the occasion? Who dined with you? What made the meal so joyful?

Think of a satisfying Mass you recently attended. What was the occasion? Who was there? What made it so joyful?

The altar and chalice at your parish church are symbols of unending delight that the Good Shepherd offers those who follow him. For what are you especially grateful today?

19. Psalm 24

In the Bible

As pilgrims approach the temple in Jerusalem, they sing of their joy. Aware of their unworthiness, they look forward to the blessings that they will receive. As they approach the area, they command the gates to grow even higher so that the Lord, the immense King of Glory, has sufficient room to take possession of his holy place.

In the Liturgy

When the community gathers at the construction site where a new church is about to be built, this psalm provides one of the options for the responsorial during the outdoor Liturgy of the Word (Chapter I). It imagines a day when the walls of the new building will rise high enough to admit the glory of God.

When the building is complete and the people have gathered outside its doors, this psalm is recommended as their processional music when they first enter the building (Chapter II). Like pilgrims of old, they may sing, "Grow higher, ancient doors. Let him enter, the king of glory."

In Your Heart
Can you recall the first time you walked through the doors of your parish church? What were you thinking on the way there? What did you anticipate before you passed through the doors?

In what other buildings have you experienced the glory of God? What made those places special?

Have you gone to a building site to imagine the future construction? What did you most anticipate there?

20. Psalm 26:8

In the Bible
The person singing this psalm declares self-innocence before God. One sign of such purity of heart is this attestation: "I love the house where you dwell, the place where your glory abides."

In the Liturgy
This is one of the options for the gospel verse at the anniversary celebration of the dedication of your parish church (Chapter VIII).

In Your Heart
What do you say when you pray for a special intention? Do you speak spontaneously or with some favorite prayers?

Do you ever declare your own innocence before God to show why you are worthy of receiving an answer to your prayers? How would you best make your argument?

What are the things you love the most about your parish church building, the place where God's glory abides?

21. Psalm 27:4

In the Bible
This psalm of trust opens with confidence in the Lord and expresses a firm desire in verse 4: "There is one thing I ask of the Lord, only this do I seek: to live in the house of the Lord all the days of my life, to gaze on the beauty of the Lord, to inquire at his temple."

In the Liturgy
This verse is one of the options for the communion antiphon on the anniversary of the dedication of the church (Chapter VIII). It expresses the worshiper's trust in God and comfort at church.

In Your Heart
Where do you wish you could live? Why there? What kind of dwelling place brings you comfort?

How do you experience the beauty of the Lord in his dwelling place, your parish church? As you celebrate its anniversary of dedication, what memories increase your desire for the building?

What have you inquired of God lately? How does the church building help you present your prayers? Your supplication implies your trust in God. Offer thanks.

22. Psalm 36:10

In the Bible
Psalm 36 contrasts the transgressions of the sinner with the mercy of God who provides proper protection and guidance.

In one popular verse, the singer acclaims to God, "For with you is the fountain of life, and in your light we see light."

In the Liturgy
When a new altar is dedicated inside a previously dedicated church, this antiphon is recommended for the lighting of its candles (Chapter IV). The bishop has prayed to God to dedicate the altar; he has anointed and incensed it. Others have stepped forward to adorn it with a cloth and surround it with flowers. Then the bishop hands the deacon a burning taper and invites him to light the altar candles. As he does, even the electrical lights above the altar may be switched on. You see light in the light of Christ.

In Your Heart
When have you experienced utter darkness? What was that like? What source of light finally rescued you?

In your home, which lights do you commonly switch on? Why those? Why do you need light in those places? What makes it possible for you to have light?

What do the altar candles of your church symbolize for you? What does it mean to see the lights of your parish church come on? When you look at the altar candles, what makes you pray, "in your light we see light"? How does this altar provide light in your life?

23. Psalm 42-43

In the Bible
Some of the same verses appear in both of these psalms, so the two are sometimes prayed together. They challenge the person who may feel downcast by recalling the hope we have in God. Verse 4 of Psalm 43 declares, "I will come to the altar of God, to God, my joy and gladness."

In the Liturgy

When the construction of a new church begins, verses from these two psalms may be used as a responsorial psalm (Chapter I). The community gathered on the building site may sing, "May your truth guide me, O Lord, to your holy mountain." They are thirsting to enter and appear before the face of God.

When an altar is to be dedicated in a previously dedicated church, this psalm may be sung at the entrance (Chapter IV). As those who made pilgrimage to the altar of Jerusalem's temple once sang in the past, so the community today may sing, "I will come to the altar of God."

At the anniversary of the dedication of the church, Psalm 43:4 is one of the recommendations for the communion antiphon.

In Your Heart

What has drawn you to the altar of your parish church? Have you had moments of joy or concern that brought you to prayer? You often pray at home, but was there some occasion when you felt you had to bring a particular intention to the altar at your church?

Think about the features of the altar in your parish church. What makes it distinctive? How does it symbolize a place of sacrifice and a table of communion?

What other places do you consider holy? What fills you with joy and gladness when you go there?

24. Psalm 45 (Hebrews 1:9)

In the Bible

This psalm was probably composed for a royal wedding and praises the bride and groom gathered in the court. Verse 8 recalls the ceremonies that conferred royalty upon the groom in the first place: "God, your God, has anointed you with the oil of gladness above other kings."

The first chapter of the New Testament letter to the Hebrews interprets the same passage as a prophecy for the mystical anointing of Christ as the Son of God.

In the Liturgy
In other contexts, Psalm 45 contributes to celebrations of the Virgin Mary, the spouse of the Holy Spirit, who gave birth to a king. In the liturgies of dedication, however, it may be sung during the anointing of the altar, together with verse 8 as its refrain. It is especially recommended for the dedication of a new altar in a previously dedicated church (Chapter IV). When the complete building is new, the bishop anoints the walls, not just the altar, so the recommended psalms and antiphons pertain to the entire church. In this liturgy, the altar is the focus, and the altar symbolizes Christ, a title that means "anointed."

In Your Heart
You were anointed at your baptism and confirmation. In what ways do you share in the oil of gladness? When have you felt most glad because of your faith?

How do you use oils in your daily life at home? How do they make you glad?

A bishop anoints a new altar of every church. At Mass, the priest and deacon kiss the altar. The priest may incense it. Ministers may bow to it. How else do people revere the altar in your parish church?

25. Psalm 46:2-3, 5-6, 8-9

In the Bible
Psalm 46 acclaims God as a refuge and strength. It proclaims that the Lord of hosts is with us as a stronghold.

In the Liturgy

The lectionary offers this psalm as one of the options for the responsorial for Mass at the dedication of a church already in use (Chapter III) or on the anniversary of the dedication of the parish church (Chapter VIII). The previous usage and endurance of the building symbolizes the presence of God, who is with his people as their refuge, strength, and stronghold.

In Your Heart

How has your parish church provided sanctuary for you? How is it a place of refuge and strength?

In what other places do you experience the presence of God? How is God with you there?

When have you especially felt the need for a stronghold in your life? When have you not felt safe? How does God provide you a refuge?

26. Psalm 48:2-4, 9-11, 13-15

In the Bible

This psalm sings the praise of God who dwells in the holy city of Jerusalem. These particular verses invite people to walk around the city to behold its greatness and to reflect upon it as a symbol of God's strength and wonder.

In the Liturgy

When the construction of a new church is about to begin, the bishop goes to bless the site (Chapter I). As he sprinkles blessed water upon the ground, all may sing these verses of Psalm 48. The bishop may walk the perimeter where the foundation will be laid, as everyone sings, "Walk through Zion, walk all around her." The church to be raised here will be an image of the holy city where God chooses to dwell.

In Your Heart

Think about the city where you live. In what ways is it the dwelling place of God? Where do you encounter God in your city? What are its strengths that can be compared to the strengths of God?

How is your parish church like a holy city? What activities take place in your parish that make it a place of interaction and growth?

If you are able, walk around the site of your future parish church. How do you anticipate it will be an image of the city where God dwells?

27. Psalm 51:21

In the Bible

In a great prayer of repentance, Psalm 51 appeals to God for mercy. At the end, the psalm asks for the restoration of fallen Jerusalem so that God may delight in "right sacrifice, burnt offerings wholly consumed."

In the Liturgy

This is one option for the communion antiphon at the Mass commemorating the anniversary of the dedication of the parish church (Chapter VIII). Those who sing it pray for the preservation of their building—not for their own benefit but that God may receive proper praise. It is recommended during communion because of its reference to right sacrifices in Jerusalem's temple.

In Your Heart

How have you witnessed the restoration of your parish church? How has the building been preserved? How have the people been renewed?

What helps you give proper praise at church? The music? The preaching? The decorations? Praise God for an environment that helps you pray.

How are you especially in communion with God today? Which of your actions this past week do you hope pleased God?

28. Psalm 65:2

In the Bible
This psalm offers a hymn of praise for the wondrous deeds of God. It was first offered in the temple of Jerusalem. The opening verse honors not just the celebrated location, but God, who deserves worship from there: "Praise is due to you in Sion, O God. To you we pay our vows in Jerusalem."

In the Liturgy
This verse may be sung during the gospel acclamation at the anniversary celebration for the dedication of the church (Chapter VIII). By recalling the praise that people offered from Jerusalem's temple, it encourages the praise of God from this church as well.

In Your Heart
For what are you especially grateful? As you give thanks to God today, what stands atop your list?

Where do you like to go to give God praise? When you go to church, where do you usually sit? Why?

How is your church like the holy city of Jerusalem? How is it a place where God dwells? How have you seen God active in your parish community? Give praise for that.

29. Psalm 68:6-7, 36

In the Bible
This psalm proclaims the triumph of God over enemies. God resides in a holy place where he acts as a father of orphans and defender of widows, a provider for the homeless and for prisoners. The psalm concludes with a powerful declaration of awe: "Wondrous is God in his holy place."

In the Liturgy
The verses of this psalm identify a holy place where God answers prayers. When sung during the liturgy, they show the holiness of the parish church. The last verse is recommended as an antiphon at the dedication of a church (Chapter II). It applies to the circumstance where the people have been unable to gather outside the building to process in together. Instead, they are already inside when the bishop arrives to begin the ceremony. As the procession of ministers enters, the people may sing, "God is in his holy place, God who unites those who dwell in his house; he himself gives might and strength to his people."

The same verse is also recommended as an entrance antiphon for the dedication of a church that has already been in use (Chapter III). God has already visited this holy place, even before its solemn dedication.

These verses may also be used as the entrance antiphon on the anniversary celebration of the dedication of the parish church (Chapter VIII). They declare that God is in the place that worshipers call their home.

In Your Heart
Imagine yourself inside your parish church and pray these words from this psalm: "Wondrous is God in his holy place."

How has God proved wondrous in the church you call your own?

Psalm 68 praises God as a patron of those who are marginalized: the orphan, the widow, the homeless, and the prisoner. How have you felt marginalized in your life? How has God provided you comfort?

What other places do you consider holy? Where else have you gone that inspires you to proclaim how wondrous God is in this holy place?

30. Psalm 84

In the Bible

A beloved pilgrimage psalm to the Jerusalem temple, this hymn praises the beauty of the building and the longing of one's heart to go there, to spend even a day there, or better yet, to live there.

In the Liturgy

Expressing the believers' love for their place of worship, this psalm appears many times in the liturgies pertaining to the dedication of a church and altar.

If the bishop leads the people in procession toward the construction site where a new church is about to be built, all may sing Psalm 84 along the way (Chapter I). Verse 3 may supply the antiphon: "My soul is longing for the courts of the Lord." The people long for their church even before it is built.

This entire psalm is recommended for the anointing of the altar and the walls of a new church (Chapters II and III). The bishop may enlist the help of priests in this task. The shimmering of the oil on the walls reflects the loveliness of the building.

In the Mass of dedication of an altar within a previously dedicated church (Chapter IV), verses 10-11 are recommended for the entrance antiphon: "Turn your eyes, O God, our shield, and look on the face of your Anointed One; one day within your courts is better than a thousand elsewhere." The Roman Gradual recommends verses 10 and 11, and then 2 and 3 as the entrance, and then verses 2-5 and 9-11 at communion on the anniversary of the dedication of the church (Chapter VIII).

At the dedication of an altar (Chapter IV), verse 4 may be sung as the communion antiphon: "The sparrow finds a home, and the swallow a nest for her young: By your altars, O Lord of hosts, my King and my God. Blessed are they who dwell in your house, for ever singing your praise."

At the dedication of an altar (Chapter IV) or at the anniversary Mass commemorating the dedication of the church (Chapter VIII), this psalm is recommended as the responsorial and at communion. It may be used as the responsorial psalm for the dedication of a church already in use (Chapter III).

In Your Heart

A church building can create strong emotions within a person. What do you feel when you think about your church? When do you most long to go to the church?

The chrism used to anoint the altar and the walls of your church make it lovely. What other features of the building do you consider lovely?

Psalm 84 compares sparrows in their nests to people in the temple. In what ways does your parish church make you feel at home?

31. Psalm 87:1-3, 4-5, 6-7

In the Bible

Psalm 87 expresses the people's pride in the holy city where God has chosen to dwell, which they call their home. Founded upon a mountain, it possesses physical security and spiritual identity.

In the Liturgy
Verses from this psalm are recommended as a responsorial for the commencement of work on the building of a church (Chapter I). As the gates of the city of Zion were set on a firm foundation, the community prays that their new building will enjoy the same strength.

In Your Heart
Our lives can be uprooted in various ways. What have you found to be the strongest foundation in your life? What keeps you centered even when security is threatened?

As the construction begins on your parish church, visit the site if you are able. Pray that the foundation laid here will symbolize the community's foundation of faith in God.

The Bible sometimes refers to God as a rock or a strong foundation. Do you have a favorite rock in some landscape that has inspired you? What are your favorite images for God? Why do they inspire you?

32. Psalm 95:1-2, 3-5, 6-7

In the Bible
The opening verses of Psalm 95 call God the rock who saves, a great king more powerful than the forces of nature. They also invite worshipers to assume different postures in God's presence: to bow, bend low, and kneel.

In the Liturgy
These verses are recommended as one option for the responsorial psalm for the dedication Mass of a church already in use (Chapter III), at the dedication of an altar inside a previously dedicated church (Chapter IV), and on the anniversary of the church's dedication (Chapter VIII).

In Your Heart

The altar of your parish church is an image of Christ and a symbol of the strength and reliability of God. How has God been a rock in your life?

You assume different postures while you pray at home and at church. What postures mean the most to you? How do they change the experience of your prayer?

When you pray at home, do you go to a favorite place? Do you assume a favorite posture? Why?

33. Psalm 96:8, 9

In the Bible

In a prayer praising the creation and salvation of God, the psalmist encourages worshipers, "Bring an offering and enter his courts; worship the Lord in holy splendor."

In the Liturgy

This is one recommendation for the communion antiphon on the anniversary of the dedication of the church (Chapter VIII). As you have entered this church many times and offered your life at Mass, so you may worship in a splendid anniversary celebration by receiving communion within the sacred place.

In Your Heart

Think about your commute to church. How do you get there? What do you bring in your hands? What do you bring in your heart as you go?

How do you worship the Lord "in holy splendor"? How does your dress give praise to God? How does the decoration of the church reflect God's glory?

Think about the people who helped build your parish church and originally celebrated its dedication. How did they sacrifice? How does your sacrifice continue their love and service?

34. Psalm 100

In the Bible
Early believers sang this psalm as they approached the end of
a pilgrimage to the Jerusalem temple. They entered the gates
of the Lord with thanksgiving and sang praise in the courts of
the temple.

In the Liturgy
At the commencement of work on the building of a new
church, this is one of the psalms recommended as the responsorial (Chapter I). It shows the longing of the people to pass
through new doors into the new church.

   When the building has been completed, and the bishop arrives to dedicate it, he may gather with the people outside the
door for a ceremony that precedes their first access to the building (Chapter II). When the moment arrives to go in, the bishop
quotes verse 4 of this psalm: "Enter the gates of the Lord with
thanksgiving, his courts with songs of praise."

In Your Heart
People naturally turn to God in times of need, but not so often
in times of thanksgiving. Yet each of us knows the warmth of
hearing words of thanks.

   For what are you thankful today? When you next arrive at
your parish church, how can you enter its gates with thanksgiving?

   Psalm 100 invites people to enter God's presence singing
for joy. When you feel the joy of God's presence, what hymn
do you like to sing?

   As you enter a church building, what helps you become
aware that you are crossing a threshold into holy ground?

35. Psalm 110:4

In the Bible

This verse from Psalm 110 quotes the Lord saying, "You are a priest forever, according to the order of Melchizedek." It recalls the mysterious figure from the book of Genesis, who appears to offer a sacrifice of bread and wine, and then disappears. The New Testament applies this verse to Jesus Christ, king and priest, who left us a memorial of the sacrifice of his life under the forms of bread and wine.

In the Liturgy

In the special preface for the dedication of a new altar in a previously dedicated church, the bishop makes an allusion to this verse (Chapter IV). He calls Christ the "true Priest." He fulfills what Melchizedek foreshadowed and what the psalm foresaw: a priest who would serve forever.

In Your Heart

This verse recalls Melchizedek as a priest who offered bread and wine. Think about the priests you have known. In what ways have they strengthened your faith? How have they helped you persevere in offering sacrifice?

When you come to Mass, you join other members of a priestly people, all of whom offer sacrifice together with the ordained priest. What sacrifices are you offering to God these days? How else do you fulfill your duty as a member of the priesthood of all the baptized?

Every Mass is ultimately celebrated by Christ the true priest. How do you experience the presence of Christ when you come to church for the Eucharist?

36. Psalm 116:10-19

In the Bible

The book of Psalms has a dual numbering system because of distinct traditions dividing the psalms from 1 to 150. Most of the psalms are one number apart in the two systems. There is a particular difficulty with Psalm 116 because some Bibles consider the first half of it as Psalm 114, and only the second half is Psalm 115. That second half contributes the verses under consideration here. It pledges trust in the Lord, especially by citing a particularly strong image in verse 13: "The cup of salvation I will raise; I will call on the name of the Lord." Verse 17 calls the offering "a thanksgiving sacrifice."

In the Liturgy

This psalm, especially verse 13, is recommended for the occasion when a priest blesses a new chalice and paten (Chapter VII). It may be sung after the new vessels are placed on the altar just before the priest approaches to pray over them. If the blessing takes place during Mass, the psalm may reappear at the preparation of the gifts. If the blessing takes place outside Mass, it may be sung as the liturgy begins. The recommended petitions of the universal prayer refer to it when it speaks about the people's thirst for "the cup of salvation."

In Your Heart

We gather at Mass to offer a thanksgiving sacrifice, and the priest uses a special cup at the altar, a chalice to be filled with the Blood of Christ.

The word "Eucharist" comes from the Greek word for "thanksgiving." When you arrive for Mass, what makes you thankful? What great deeds of God fill your heart with gratitude?

The chalice of the Blood of Christ is the cup of salvation. Why do you need salvation? What do you need to be saved from? Is there something pulling you away from the saving streams of the Blood of Christ?

37. Psalm 118

In the Bible
This psalm of praise thanks God who has offered rescue. The singer promises to enter the gates of righteousness to thank the Lord (verse 19) and marvels that the stone rejected by the builders has become the cornerstone (verse 22).

In the Liturgy
At the commencement of work on a new church building, or when the bishop comes to dedicate a new altar in a previously dedicated church, verses of this psalm offer one possibility for the responsorial (Chapter I and Chapter IV). The reference to the cornerstone, which the New Testament interprets as a foreshadowing of Christ, is especially fitting.

During the anointing of the new altar in a previously dedicated church, this entire psalm may be sung along with the refrain "The stone which the builders rejected has become the cornerstone" (Chapter IV).

In Your Heart
How is Christ the cornerstone of your life? Have you experienced times when you rejected him, only to discover that he has always been your rock of strength?

How does the altar of your church represent Christ for you? How does its location in the building focus your attention at the Mass? What are your favorite memories of a church altar? Why?

How do people rely on you as the rock of their lives? How are you an altar of sacrifice for the sake of the people you love?

38. Psalm 119:105a, 129, 130, 133, 135, 144

In the Bible
The longest psalm in the Bible, Psalm 119 slowly and deliberately meditates on the Word of God. Alphabetic in structure, its sections contain verses that all begin with successive letters of the Hebrew alphabet.

In the Liturgy
The lectionary frequently plucks samples from Psalm 119, seeking out specific verses that cohere—not because of the alphabet but because of a specific interior theme. At the dedication of an altar in a previously dedicated church, these verses are recommended as one option for the responsorial psalm (Chapter IV). The refrain calls God's Word a lamp for one's feet, a light on one's path (105a). The other verses deal with light and guidance.

In Your Heart
How have you let the Word of God enlighten your path? Can you think of a time when the world seemed dark to you, but a passage from the Bible shed the light you most needed? Which passage was it?

Laws sometimes feel restrictive, but they are created for guidance. You are a citizen of a great country, residing in a municipality. What civil laws make you proud? Which ones provide light?

Candles are lighted at the altar of your church. They provide more than light and heat. What do they symbolize for you? What connections do you see between the symbols of altar and light?

39. Psalm 122

In the Bible
A great pilgrimage psalm to the Jerusalem temple, this hymn captures the joy of those who have made a long journey from

their homes to the dwelling place of God. It praises the unity that believers experience upon arriving together in the holy city, and it prays for peace there.

In the Liturgy
Predictably, this is one of the most popular psalms in the various rites of dedication of a church and altar. It captures the joy of believers entering their house of prayer.

At the dedication of a new church, Psalm 122 is the recommended chant as the procession enters the church for the first time (Chapter II). Even if the church being dedicated has already enjoyed some usage, this psalm may begin the celebration (Chapter III).

If an altar is being dedicated in a previously dedicated church, Psalm 122 may be used as the responsorial (Chapter IV).

At the dedication of a church already in use (Chapter III) or on the annual celebration of the dedication of the parish church (Chapter VIII), it may be the responsorial psalm for the Liturgy of the Word. The first verse may be sung in the gospel acclamation of the anniversary day, and verses 3 and 4 are an option for the communion antiphon.

In Your Heart
Can you recall a time when you made a long pilgrimage to a holy place? Where was it? What did you feel when you arrived?

Your parish gathers many different people for worship. You may not have much in common with some of them, but all of you share belief. Think about the other people who worship with you under one roof. What makes you united?

Psalm 122 concludes with a prayer for the peace of Jerusalem. Peace is important for your parish as well. How do you contribute to the peace that people experience there? What more can you do to provide a sanctuary of peace?

40. Psalm 125:2-3

In the Bible
This prayer contrasts the lot of the wicked with those who put their trust in God. The faithful are like Mount Sion, "that cannot be shaken, that stands forever." The Lord surrounds his people like the mountains around Jerusalem.

In the Liturgy
This is one option for a verse that may be sung before the gospel of the anniversary celebration of the dedication of the parish church during Lent (Chapter VIII). Those who have worshiped in this house have experienced God's protection. The people who worshiped in Jerusalem's temple felt the same way.

In Your Heart
As you think over your experiences inside your parish church, how have you felt God's protection?

How have you witnessed God's unshakable presence in your life? How has God been like mountains around you?

What is happening in your life right now that causes you to put your trust in God? How does that feel?

41. Psalm 128

In the Bible
This prayer about family life opens by proclaiming blessed those who fear the Lord. A husband and wife behold God's blessing in their many children gathered "like shoots of the olive" around the family table. The psalm concludes with a prayer for Israel's peace.

In the Liturgy
All the principal liturgies of dedication recommend Psalm 128 for communion: the dedication of a new church (Chapter II), the dedication of a church already in use (Chapter III), and the dedication of a new altar in a previously dedicated church (Chapter IV). As the children in the psalm reveal God's blessings upon their family gathered at the table, so the children of the church show God's blessings upon the parish when they gather at the new altar.

In Your Heart
Think about the table where you eat your meals. Who shares it with you? Who shared a family table with you in the past? Thank God for the blessings of those who dine with you.

Think about those who gather around the altar at your parish church. They too are signs of God's blessings. Offer a prayer of gratitude for the blessings you have received through those who share your faith in this community.

What other activities do you perform with those who eat with you? Do you play together? Serve together? Learn together? How does this apply to those who eat and drink with you at the Eucharist?

42. Psalm 130:7

In the Bible
The person singing this psalm is aware of personal sin, but also of the "great power to redeem" that the Lord possesses.

In the Liturgy
At the anniversary Mass for the dedication of the church (Chapter VIII), the priest alludes to Malachi 1:11 when he prays in the collect that "in this place . . . there may always be pure

worship" for God. In the same prayer, referring to Psalm 130:7, he asks that the people may receive "fullness of redemption."

In Your Heart

How have you experienced God's power to redeem? When have you been brought low, only to be raised up again?

As you celebrate the anniversary of the dedication of your parish church, how has your community experienced God's great power to redeem? How has God built up the parish over the years?

Many apostles and saints have gone through a personal conversion. Which of them have inspired your journey of faith? Which stories of sin and redemption have consoled you the most?

43. Psalm 138

In the Bible

This prayer of gratitude still captures the hearts of believers today. It opens with the words "I thank you, Lord, with all my heart." It gives special praise to God, who answers prayers. The believer who first sang this psalm went to the temple to offer thanks "in the presence of the angels." Prayer at home was not enough.

In the Liturgy

In the dedication ceremonies, when the bishop incenses the new altar, Psalm 138 is recommended (Chapters II, III, and IV). The altar will become the central place for the prayer of thanksgiving, the eucharistic prayer. Angelic hosts at the altar unite their voices with those of the local community to sing "Holy, holy, holy." The dedication liturgy pairs Psalm 138 with verses from the book of Revelation about an angel with a golden censer at the altar of God (8:3-4). The parish community prays in thanksgiving at its new altar, surrounded by clouds of incense that recall the honor God receives from all creation in heaven and on earth.

The prayer after communion at the dedication Mass makes a reference to this psalm. The biblical verse expresses one's desire to adore God in the holy temple in the sight of the angels. The bishop prays after communion "that we may constantly adore you in your holy temple and glory in your sight with all the Saints" (Chapters II and III).

The same psalm is recommended as the offertory chant for the anniversary celebration of the dedication of the parish church (Chapter VIII). In the same celebration, verse 2 may be sung with the gospel acclamation.

In Your Heart

For what are you most thankful today? Try praying Psalm 138 with that in mind.

At every Mass, the eucharistic prayer opens with a preface offering reasons for giving God thanks. When the priest commands you to lift up your heart, you have an opportunity to thank God at the altar. The next time you hear a preface, think about your personal reasons for giving thanks.

On certain occasions, the priest incenses the gifts of bread and wine, the altar and the cross. The aroma fills the church as the smoke rises to the heavens, mixing with the praise of angels. As you pray, "Holy, holy, holy" with the angels, imagine their voices blending with your prayers of thanksgiving.

44. Psalm 141:2

In the Bible

The believer who sings this psalm prays, "Let my prayer be as incense before you, the raising of my hands like an evening oblation." It shows the desire to offer an aromatic sacrifice that will please God.

In the Liturgy
The bishop alludes to this verse when he lights the incense at the newly dedicated altar for the first time (Chapters II, III, and IV). He prays, "Let our prayer rise, O Lord, like incense in your sight, and as this house is filled with a pleasing fragrance, so let your Church be fragrant with the aroma of Christ."

In Your Heart
What are your favorite fragrances? In your home, which aromas are most pleasing? What do those smells mean to you?

Are there smells you associate with certain places? What causes them? What do those aromas mean to you?

Imagine that God can smell your prayer. Is it a pleasing aroma? What could you say that would raise your prayer to God like incense?

45. Psalm 147:12-20

In the Bible
The book of Psalms confuses some people because the numbering of the psalms follows two different systems. Psalm 23 in one Bible is Psalm 22 in another. The two systems rejoin in these verses of Psalm 147. They invite Jerusalem to give thanks to God for reasons that include filling the city with "finest wheat."

In the Liturgy
If the newly dedicated church has a separate chapel for the tabernacle with the Blessed Sacrament, the bishop inaugurates it by carrying a ciborium of consecrated hosts there at

the conclusion of communion (Chapters II and III). All may sing these verses of Psalm 147 with the refrain, "O Jerusalem, glorify the Lord." The key verse that makes it appropriate is the one about "finest wheat," a prophetic description of the Body of Christ under the form of bread.

These verses are also recommended at communion time for the anniversary celebration of the dedication of your church (Chapter VIII).

In Your Heart
Wheat fields are a sign of the productive earth. What crops grow near your home? How are they signs of God's goodness to you?

Wheat is cut and ground to make flour. Is flour used much in your kitchen? What kind of flour? What food products do you most enjoy that make you aware of the finest that God has to offer? Thank God for your food and the farmers who grow it.

As you receive communion in your church, thank God for the blessing of productive soil that makes bread possible. A consecrated host is small and may not have much flavor, but it is the finest wheat.

46. Isaiah 12:3

In the Bible
The prophet brings hope to the people by promising them a day when they will draw water from the springs of salvation and give thanks to the Lord, making his deeds known among the nations.

In the Liturgy
When the bishop dedicates a new altar in a previously dedicated church, he offers a special preface at the beginning of

the eucharistic prayer (Chapter IV). This passage is one of several that lie behind this statement: "Here the faithful drink of your Spirit from the streams that flow from Christ." This altar will provide the source of the life-giving Blood of Christ, from which the people drink the mystery of their salvation, fulfilling the prophecy of Isaiah.

When the bishop blesses a movable altar or one for use in a chapel or oratory, he offers a special prayer (Chapter V and VI). He asks God, "let it be the fountain from which flows an unending stream of salvation."

In Your Heart
Recall a time when you were very thirsty. What conditions caused it? What finally brought you relief?

What is your own regular source of water? When have you been most aware of it? Give God thanks for the water that brings you life.

The water of your baptism was the original spring of salvation for you. When you drink the Blood of Christ, you receive from another spring of salvation. Why do you think Jesus asked his disciples to drink his Blood? What does that signify for you?

47. Isaiah 28:16-17

In the Bible
Isaiah prophesies a better day for Israel's leadership, declaring that God will lay a stone in Jerusalem, a precious cornerstone as a sure foundation. The future leadership will be as steady as a strong building. This passage is also cited in 1 Peter 2:6.

In the Liturgy
This is one of the scriptural passages suggested for the reading at the commencement of work on building a new church (Chapter I). Especially if the cornerstone is being laid, this

makes an appropriate selection. People will see Isaiah's words as a prophecy for Christ, the cornerstone of their faith, represented by this future church.

In Your Heart
Think about the strong leaders you have had in your family, work, church, or society. What made them like cornerstones?

Who is the cornerstone of your life today? Why?

In what ways does your parish church provide a firm foundation for you and your family? How does it provide solid leadership and reliable strength?

48. Isaiah 54:12

In the Bible
Isaiah prophesies a better day for the exiled people of Jerusalem, who lost their temple, the center of their worship and of their lives. "All your walls will be of precious stones and the towers of Jerusalem built with gems."

In the Liturgy
When the bishop sprinkles blessed water on the ground where a future church is about to be built, the people may sing this verse together with Psalm 48 (Chapter I). It envisions a beautiful building worthy of giving God praise.

In Your Heart
What items in your personal possession are precious to you? Do you have stones or gems that you treasure? What do they mean for you?

What makes a church building beautiful? When you think of the exterior walls of churches you know, which ones stand out for their beauty? Why?

Providing beauty in a public place like a church gives praise to God and inspires everyone. In what ways is your parish a treasure that is open to the community? Who are the groups that find a home within its precious walls? How are those people like gems that make your church beautiful?

49. Isaiah 56:1, 6-7 (Matthew 21:13; Mark 11:17; Luke 19:46)

In the Bible
Isaiah urges the people to do what is right and promises that God's salvation will come to deliver them. God promises to bring even foreigners into the holy mountain of Jerusalem, where their offerings will be accepted on his altar, "for my house shall be called a house of prayer for all peoples."

In the Liturgy
At the dedication of a new church, Isaiah 56:7 is one of the passages that inspired the suggested communion antiphon: "My house shall be a house of prayer, says the Lord" (Chapters II and III). Jesus quoted that passage from Isaiah when he cleansed the temple (Matthew 21:13; Mark 11:17; Luke 19:46). The verse reminds those who are sharing communion that they have reached a moment in the ceremony that explains the holiness of this church. The same antiphon may be sung at communion on the anniversary of the dedication (Chapter VIII).

At the beginning of the dedication of an altar (Chapter IV), the entrance antiphon may come from Isaiah 59:21 and Isaiah 56:7. God promises that his words will remain forever and that acceptable sacrifices will be offered on the altar. The community gives thanks that this prophecy is being fulfilled even in their parish church.

At the dedication of a church already in use (Chapter III) or on the dedication anniversary celebration (Chapter VIII), this passage may serve as the first reading for the Mass.

At the end of the dedication or blessing of a new church, the bishop offers a solemn blessing (Chapters II, III, and V). He prays that the people "may be made thoroughly clean, so that God may dwell within" them. As the temple was cleansed, so the people who are God's house are to be clean. The same blessing occurs at the end of the Mass on the anniversary of the dedication (Chapter VIII).

In Your Heart

Jesus used this passage from Isaiah to declare that the temple was set aside for prayer. What different types of prayer have you experienced in your parish church? What events do you recall that especially made your building a place for worship?

At what times in your life have you especially felt drawn to your church because it is a house of prayer? How has it fulfilled your needs?

As each year passes, your parish community gives thanks to God for the dedication of its church. God has surely been pleased with the offerings there. What significant ceremonies did you experience at church over the past year? How has it been a house of prayer for all peoples?

50. Isaiah 59:21

In the Bible

God promises that the covenant will remain forever. The spirit he placed upon the people and the words he put into their mouths will remain with them and with their children—and their children's children.

In the Liturgy

The entrance antiphon for the dedication of an altar (IV) may come from Isaiah 59:21 and Isaiah 56:7. In chapter 59, God promises that his words will remain forever, passed down from one generation to the next. The community gives thanks that this prophecy is being fulfilled even in their parish church.

In Your Heart

In your family, has God's Word echoed from one generation to the next? From whom did you first learn about your faith?

In your parish family, how is the prophecy of Isaiah being fulfilled? Can you think of a family of several generations within your community?

What ministries in your parish help pass the faith from one generation to the next? How can you support them?

51. Isaiah 60:1, 3

In the Bible

The people living in exile have experienced a time of spiritual darkness. Through the prophet Isaiah, God promises them light. The glory of the Lord will rise upon them, and other nations will walk by the light of God's own people.

In the Liturgy

These verses are recommended for the dedication of a new church (Chapters II and III). As the ministers light the candles on the altar and walls for the first time, the people may sing, "Your light has come, Jerusalem." This lighting is not just for the practical needs of the people inside the building on an overcast day. It symbolizes their responsibility to evangelize, so that the nations will walk in their light.

In Your Heart
How will your new parish church serve as a light for those who are not members of the community? What will they notice when they pass by? What will strike their attention when they enter?

How are the members of your parish community a light for others? What activities taking place on or off site are spreading the light of Christ?

How do people come to know Christ through you? How does God use you as his light to lead others out of darkness?

52. Isaiah 66:1

In the Bible
The Lord proclaims that heaven is his throne, the earth his footstool. He rhetorically asks the people intent on building a holy temple what house they could possibly build for him.

In the Liturgy
At the dedication of a new church (Chapters II and III) and on the anniversary of the dedication of the parish church (Chapter VIII), this verse may be sung during the gospel acclamation. It keeps people humble who may otherwise be proud of their own accomplishments building a church. It reminds them that God owns the cosmos.

In Your Heart
In the created world, where do you most encounter the presence of God? What are your favorite places to experience God outdoors?

How is your parish church a place where God dwells? How have you experienced God's special presence in your church over the past year?

Given the vastness of the universe, meditate on the amazing presence of God in your local community and in your personal life.

53. Jeremiah 30:18

In the Bible
Through the prophet Jeremiah, God speaks to a people who were driven into exile and whose city had been destroyed. God promises to bring them home and rebuild Jerusalem upon its mound.

In the Liturgy
When the bishop dedicates a new altar in a previously dedicated building, he offers a special preface at the beginning of the eucharistic prayer (Chapter IV). Referring to the altar, he prays, "Truly this is an exalted place," a reference to the reconstruction of Jerusalem upon its mound. His prayer also invites a connection to the hill of Calvary, where Christ offered his life on the altar of the cross.

In Your Heart
Inside a Catholic church, the altar usually sits on a raised area, not just so that it may be seen, but so that it may be exalted. In the design of your parish church, which parts are higher than the rest? Why?

When you climb any hill or a tower, you get a different view. Where are the places that you have most liked to climb? Why? How have they helped your perspective on life?

Have you personally experienced a time of loss and restoration? What was the "mound" upon which God rebuilt your life? How do you see better from there? Why does it feel like home?

54. Ezekiel 36:22-26

In the Bible
To a people who have polluted their lives by worshiping false gods, God promises to sprinkle clean water upon them and give them a new spirit. He will remove their stony heart and give them a natural heart.

In the Liturgy
When the bishop arrives to bless a newly built church, he sprinkles blessed water upon the people and the building (Chapter II). The action purifies the walls and the altar for the sacred ceremonies that will take place there, but it also reminds the people of their baptism and prepares them for worship. One of the antiphons that the people may sing especially during Lent comes from Ezekiel: "I will pour clean water upon you."

The same antiphon may be used during a sprinkling rite in Lent for the dedication of a church already in use and of a new altar in a previously dedicated church (Chapters III and IV). It may also be used for the blessing of a church serving as a chapel or oratory (Chapter V).

In Your Heart
How have you experienced the cleansing waters of God's mercy? How were you able to move from sinful behavior in the past, through forgiveness, and into a person newly committed to Christ?

How has water played an important role in your life? You need it for drink. You use it for cleansing. You were baptized in water. How else has water been part of your personal history?

Even now, are there times when you sadly discover that you have a heart of stone? How can the use of blessed water help you receive a heart of flesh?

55. Ezekiel 37:27

In the Bible
God promises his exiled people that his dwelling place shall be with them. They will be his people. He will be their God.

In the Liturgy
When the bishop arrives to bless a building site where work is commencing, the people gather to pray with him (Chapter I). During the readings from Scripture, one of the passages that may serve as the responsorial is Psalm 100, coupled with this refrain, based on Ezekiel: "My dwelling place shall be among the people."

When the bishop dedicates a new church (Chapters II and III) or a new altar in a previously dedicated church (Chapter IV), or when the people gather to celebrate the anniversary of their church's dedication (Chapter VIII), a cantor may sing this verse in the gospel acclamation.

In Your Heart
If you are attending the blessing of a new site for your parish church, you may reflect upon God's promise that his dwelling place will be among his people. As you look forward to a new building, how do you hope God will dwell there?

How does God already dwell among the people of your parish? What virtues do you notice among them that show the influence of the Gospel in their lives?

On the anniversary of the dedication of your church, think about the past year. How has God dwelled within this church? How has God dwelled within the people who worship there? How has God dwelled with you and claimed you as his own?

56. Ezekiel 43:1-2, 4-7a

In the Bible

The temple has been destroyed. The people are in exile. God's glory has left Jerusalem. In Ezekiel's vision, however, God brings him to the gate of the temple, where he hears the glory of God returning. The spirit lifts Ezekiel up, brings him to the inner court, and the glory of God fills the temple again. The prophet hears the voice of God declaring that this place is his throne that shall never again be defiled.

In the Liturgy

When the bishop comes to bless the site where work on the construction of a new church is beginning, he closes the ceremony with a prayer (Chapter I). He asks the people to pray not only for the future building but that God will make them "the living temple of his glory." As the glory of God once came to the temple of Jerusalem, so may it fill the people who are the temple of the church.

At the dedication of a church already in use (Chapter III) or on the anniversary of the dedication of the church (Chapter VIII), this passage may be proclaimed as the first reading. It reminds people how God's glory came to rest in the sacred space of their church.

At the anniversary, in the prayer over the offerings, the priest invites the Lord to recall the day "when you were pleased to fill your house with glory and holiness" (Chapter VIII). His prayer shows that this parish church stands in a long tradition dating back to the Jerusalem temple. It too is a place where God has chosen to abide.

In Your Heart

You have entered many church buildings in your life. Each of them is a dwelling place of God. Which ones stand out in your memory? How have you experienced the glory of God inside a church?

Have you ever felt exiled from the glory of God? When have you struggled to discern God's presence?

You are God's temple. How has the Holy Spirit filled your life with glory? How might people better perceive the glory of God in your words and deeds?

57. Ezekiel 47:1-2, 8-9, 12

In the Bible
In a prophetic vision, Ezekiel finds himself at the entrance to the temple, where he sees water flowing from its sides, providing life, nourishment, and healing for all.

In the Liturgy
At the dedication of a church already in use (Chapter III) or on the anniversary of a church's dedication (Chapter VIII), this passage may be proclaimed as the first reading. It shows the purposes of a house of worship even today: providing a source of life, nourishment, and healing, especially through the sacred use of water.

When a church is dedicated, the bishop sprinkles water on the people, the altar, and the walls (Chapter II and III). Verses 1 and 9 of this passage supply one of the antiphons that the people may sing as they behold water flowing within their holy place. The same antiphons are used for the sprinkling ceremony when the bishop dedicates an altar in a previously dedicated church (Chapter IV).

In Your Heart
How do the waters of life flow from your parish church? How have you received spiritual nourishment from entering the building?

At a sprinkling rite, you recall your own baptism. What effect has baptism had in your life? How have you been purified again through the sacraments and prayers of the church?

How has water provided you a source of life and healing? How has your parish church helped you appreciate this?

58. Daniel 2:45

In the Bible
Daniel interprets the dream of Nebuchadnezzar. One of its elements is a stone cut from a mountain without the aid of human hands. Daniel interprets it as a powerful force that God alone unleashed.

In the Liturgy
When construction begins on a new church, the bishop may come to bless the cornerstone (Chapter I). When he prays over the stone, he recalls this passage from Daniel and applies it to Jesus Christ, born of a virgin, appearing among us by the action of God, "as the stone from the mountain not cut by any hand."

At the end of the same liturgy, the people pray the universal prayer. The last suggested petition names all the believers present "as living stones hewn and dressed by God's hand." The mysterious stone in the book of Daniel foreshadows not only Christ the cornerstone but the people who are living stones.

In Your Heart
How have you experienced God's mysterious presence in your life? Can you think of a time where events turned in such a way that you could only explain them as happening at the hand of God?

Consider the cornerstone of your parish church. How is Christ the rock of your parish's life? How does his divine presence reassure you in times of trouble?

How are you a rock cut by God's own hand? How has God used you to bring his message to the world?

59. Daniel 9:4, 17, 19

In the Bible
At the destruction of Jerusalem and its temple, Daniel offers a prayer of repentance on behalf of the people, asking the Lord to let his face shine upon his own sanctuary.

In the Liturgy
This is one of the passages recommended for the offertory antiphon at the anniversary celebration for the dedication of the parish church (Chapter VIII). It appears, not because of its vision of desolation, but because it asks God to look upon the prayers offered in the sanctuary. Nonetheless, if the parish has come through a difficult time, this passage may make an appropriate choice.

In Your Heart
If you take an honest look at the history of your parish church, you may recall times of great achievements and times of missed opportunities. What are your key memories of your church? Why do those stand out in your mind?

Daniel envisions the face of God shining upon the sanctuary that needs help. What parts of your parish's present or future seem unclear? What would you like God's face to illumine?

When have you experienced loss? How has the faithfulness of God seen you through?

60. Malachi 1:11

In the Bible
The Lord of Hosts speaks through the prophet Malachi to a people who have turned away from the covenant and toward

false worship. He commands that a pure offering be made in every place to his name, which is great among the nations from the rising to the setting of the sun.

In the Liturgy

Many Catholics are accustomed to hearing an echo of this verse near the beginning of Eucharistic Prayer III. The dedication of an altar in a previously dedicated church alludes to the same passage (Chapter IV). The preface of the eucharistic prayer calls the altar the place where the sacrifice of Christ is offered and where perfect praise is rendered to God.

At the anniversary Mass for the dedication of the church (Chapter VIII), the priest prays in the collect that "in this place . . . there may always be pure worship" for God. He also prays that the people may receive "fullness of redemption," an allusion to Psalm 130:7.

In Your Heart

God has commanded that a pure offering be made to his name. How do you offer your life to God? Which of your actions within your family or your place of work give glory to God's name?

Your parish church regularly celebrates the sacrifice of the Mass. How else does your parish community sacrifice? What actions and events are a pure offering to the name of the Lord from the rising of the sun to its setting?

Which "false gods" have you had to avoid? Which temptations continue to lure you away from your calling as a Christian? How can you offer a pure sacrifice?

New Testament

61. Matthew 5:14

In the Bible
During the Sermon on the Mount, Jesus proclaims to his disciples that they are the light of the world. Like a city on a hill, they cannot be hid.

In the Liturgy
When the bishop dedicates a new church, he offers a special prayer of dedication (Chapters II and III). It explores many images, including two that refer back to this passage from Matthew. He says that "this house brings to light the mystery of the Church," and he calls the church "a City set high on a mountain for all to see."

In Your Heart
Is your new church located on a physical hill? Is it noted for its height? How do people notice it when they pass by?

How is your parish like a city on a hill? How is it a light? What activities in your community proclaim to others that you are disciples of Jesus Christ?

How does light shine through you? When people look to you, how do you want them to see Christ? In what way has Christ made you his own light, his city on a hill?

62. Matthew 5:23-24

In the Bible

Jesus commands respectful behavior among his disciples. In the Sermon on the Mount, he tells them to make peace with one another before they come to offer their gift in worship at the altar.

In the Liturgy

When the bishop comes to dedicate an altar in a previously dedicated church, this passage may be proclaimed as the gospel of the Mass (Chapter IV).

Later in the same ceremony, when members of the faithful first process to the newly dedicated altar with the gifts for the Liturgy of the Eucharist, all may sing this antiphon: "If you offer your gift at the altar, and there recall that your brother has something against you, leave your gift before the altar, go first and be reconciled with your brother, and then you shall come and offer your gift, alleluia."

The same antiphon may be sung during the preparation of the gifts at a Mass when the church is being blessed as a new chapel or oratory (Chapter V) or when a movable altar is being blessed for a similar purpose (Chapter VI).

In Your Heart

Jesus commanded peace among those who offered worship at the altar. Think about the members of your parish community. Many of them are your friends because you share values and interests. Are there some with whom you disagree? What attitude does Christ ask you to possess during the procession of the gifts at every Mass?

Perhaps you have never been able to reconcile with someone. You find it difficult to make peace with a person before offering your gift. Pray for that person's well-being. Pray for peace in that person's heart.

What is the gift that you are offering at the altar? How do you practice love of neighbor? What specific act of charity can you offer the next time you participate at Mass?

63. Matthew 7:8; Luke 11:10

In the Bible

While encouraging his disciples to prayer during his Sermon on the Mount, Jesus tells them that everyone who asks receives and the door will be opened to those who knock upon it.

In the Liturgy

At the dedication of a new church, this passage forms part of a recommended communion antiphon (Chapters II and III). It joins with another passage from Isaiah, "My house shall be a house of prayer," to reassure people that when they pray there, "the one who seeks finds." The same antiphon may be sung at the anniversary Mass for the dedication of the church (Chapter VIII).

At the dedication of a church (Chapters II and III) and at anniversary Mass for the dedication of the church (Chapter VIII), this verse may be sung in the gospel acclamation.

In Your Heart

At the Eucharist, we thank God for the blessings we have received. When have you experienced an answer to your prayers? When have you knocked and found the door of your parish church opening to you?

How does your parish community commit itself to prayer? What are the occasions on which you gather for worship? What intentions do you frequently make?

Can you recall a time when you were reluctant to ask for something, but then got a quick and generous response? What does that tell you about God's generosity? How is God inviting you to be generous?

64. Matthew 7:21-29

In the Bible
During the Sermon on the Mount, Jesus gives his listeners some practical advice on discipleship. If they act on the words they hear, they are like the wise man who built his house on rock. It does not collapse in the worst of weather.

In the Liturgy
When a new church is under construction, this passage comes immediately to mind (Chapter I). It may be used as the gospel reading at the blessing of the site.

In the same ceremony, when the stonemason fixes the cornerstone in place, all may sing an antiphon from verse 24: "The house of the Lord is founded firmly, on solid rock."

At the conclusion of the same ceremony, the people offer the universal prayer. One of the suggested petitions asks that God will "set firmly on the solid rock of his Church" all those committed to the construction of the new church.

In Your Heart
How have you set your faith on the solid rock of the teachings of Christ? Can you recall a time when you held firm against the storms raging around you?

Your new church is to be built on a firm physical foundation. How have you experienced the fountain of faith in the people of your parish community? How do they follow Christ in times of trial?

As you watch the construction of your new house of worship, how are you praying that God will set you firmly on the solid rock of his church? How will you express your faith in the teachings of Christ as part of this parish?

65. Matthew 16:13-19

In the Bible

At Caesarea-Philippi, Jesus asked his disciples who people say that he is. Peter responded, "You are the Messiah, the Son of the living God." Jesus promised to build his church upon the rock of Peter.

In the Liturgy

At the beginning of work on a new church, this is one of the options for the gospel that may be proclaimed (Chapter I). As the people gather outside with their bishop, they may hear about the rock of Peter's faith.

The same passage may be proclaimed as the gospel at the dedication of a church (Chapters II and III) or at the anniversary Mass for the dedication (Chapter VIII). Verse 18, where Jesus proclaims Peter as the rock, may be used in the gospel acclamation for the same celebrations. It is the recommended offertory antiphon for the anniversary Mass (Chapter VIII).

In Your Heart

The Catholic Church sees in this passage the founding of the church upon Peter and his successors. How have you come to know Christ through the leaders of the church, especially your bishop and your pope?

How has your parish church provided you an image of rock-solid faith? How has your community helped you in times of doubt or fear?

You are a disciple of Jesus, even as Peter was. Christ is building his church upon the rock of your faith. How have you shared your faith with others? How do they know that you are a disciple?

66. Matthew 18:10

In the Bible
In a discourse to his disciples, Jesus talks about the faith of children. He says, "their angels continually see the face of my Father in heaven."

In the Liturgy
As the bishop concludes the Mass of the dedication of a new church, he offers the prayer after communion (Chapters II and III). He asks God that those who have received the heavenly gifts of the Body and Blood of Christ "may constantly adore you in your holy temple . . . with all the Saints." The bishop thus makes an allusion to this passage, praying that the community may someday adore God with the angels and saints in the heavenly temple, of which this new church is but a sign.

In Your Heart
This brief passage is also proclaimed when the church celebrates the Mass of the Guardian Angels on October 2. How have you felt the protection of God in your life? How have the angels who see God's face guarded you from danger?

Your participation in the Mass at your parish church foreshadows the participation we all hope to experience in the heavenly banquet. How is this so? What are the best qualities of the celebration of the Eucharist that give you a vision of life after death?

How do you make time to adore God? The bishop's prayer expresses the hope that we will adore God constantly in heaven. How is your time of private prayer a source of joy and peace for you?

67. Matthew 18:20

In the Bible
Jesus promised that he would be present to his disciples whenever even two or three of them were gathered in his name.

In the Liturgy
When the bishop blesses a new church to be used as a chapel
or oratory, he begins the liturgy with a special collect (Chapter
V). He asks that all who gather in this new building "may know
the presence of Jesus Christ, who promised to be in the midst
of all who are gathered in his name."

In Your Heart
Think of a time when you prayed with just two or three people,
either at home or at church—or even in some other place. How
did you experience the presence of Christ?

Sometimes you may be disappointed in the number of
people who show up for an event in your community. Can
you think of a time when Christ was especially present even
among the few who joined you in prayer?

How might Christ be calling on you to pray in community?
Perhaps you pray already in private, but are there some people
with whom you could spend more time in prayer? Who are
they? When could that happen?

68. Matthew 20:20-28

In the Bible
The mother of the sons of Zebedee asked Jesus to bestow favors on her children. Jesus asked them if they were able to
drink of the cup that he was about to drink. They would share
his suffering, but the Father alone bestows favors.

In the Liturgy
This is one of the gospel passages that may be proclaimed when a priest blesses a new chalice and paten (Chapter VII). It reminds him and all who drink the Blood of Christ what is the cost of discipleship.

In Your Heart
Have you ever asked God for favors on behalf of people in your family? Has God required something of you? Of them?

When have you drunk the cup of suffering because of your faith in Christ? Have you been ridiculed? What helped you keep strong in your faith?

As a new chalice is put into use in your community, it will become the cup of the Blood of Christ. What does it mean for you to eat and drink communion at Mass? How does it bring you comfort? How does it challenge you?

69. Matthew 26:39

In the Bible
In the Garden of Gethsemane, knowing that the end of his earthly life was near, Jesus prayed for the cup of suffering to pass him by. He prayed more that the Father's will be done.

In the Liturgy
In the unusual circumstance when a priest blesses a new chalice and paten outside of Mass, the ceremony recommends petitions for the universal prayer (Chapter VII). One of these addresses Christ as the Savior of us all "who in obedience to the will of the Father drank the chalice of suffering for our salvation."

In Your Heart
Your responsibilities sometimes call you to perform actions of great sacrifice. When did you recently face a situation that you

wished you could have avoided? How was it like Jesus' request to let the cup pass him by?

Jesus accepted the cross for the salvation of the world. How has his suffering inspired you? How has it saved you? What is God's will for you? Can you pray obediently that God's will be done?

When you see the chalice at Mass brought to the altar, raised up, and serving communion, how does it remind you of Jesus in the Garden of Gethsemane? How does it strengthen you?

70. Mark 12:1-12

In the Bible
Near the end of his life, Jesus tells the disturbing parable of the wicked tenants in the vineyard. At its climax, those entrusted with the vineyard kill the owner's son. Jesus cites a verse from Psalm 118 to apply the parable to himself: The stone that the builders rejected has become the cornerstone.

In the Liturgy
As work commences on a new church building, the bishop arrives at the site to bless it (Chapter I). This passage is one of the gospels recommended for the ceremony.

In Your Heart
Wicked people continue to perform evil deeds. How has the wickedness of others afflicted your life? What has been your source of strength?

When you meditate on the crucifixion and resurrection of Jesus, you see how the stone rejected by the builders became the cornerstone. Have you been dwelling too much on the cross in your life and not enough on the resurrection? Where could you find hope?

As the construction of your new church begins, think about the people who made it possible. Who are some individuals you were not expecting to assist in this project? Thank God for them.

71. Mark 14:12-16, 22-26

In the Bible
At the Last Supper, Jesus took a cup, gave thanks, and gave it to the disciples. They all drank from it.

In the Liturgy
When a priest blesses a new chalice and paten, this passage may serve as one of the Scripture readings (Chapter VII). It recalls the original sharing of the Blood of Christ from a cup.

In Your Heart
Place yourself at the Last Supper with the disciples. Imagine Jesus inviting you to take a sip from a common cup. Imagine him saying, "This is my Blood." What are you feeling? Why?

On the night before he died, Jesus shared the sacrament of his Body and Blood. The very loss of his life became the means of bestowing life on others. How have you experienced sacrifice and redemption? Who are the people who impressed you with their sacrifice? How have they influenced your life?

At Mass, the chalice being blessed will continue to hold the Blood of Christ, inviting you into an experience of the upper room and of Calvary. How does drinking the Blood of Christ enrich your experience of communion?

72. Luke 2:32

In the Bible
When Mary and Joseph brought their newborn son to the temple to present him to the Lord, Simeon took the child into his arms and proclaimed him "a light for revelation to the Gentiles" and for the glory of Israel.

In the Liturgy
At the dedication of a new church, candles are lighted just after the dedication of the altar (Chapters II and III). These new candles remind the community that Christ is a light for revelation to the Gentiles, whose brightness shines in the church and upon the whole human family. The same is true when candles are lighted at the dedication of a new altar in a previously dedicated church (Chapter IV).

In Your Heart
Think about the placement of lamps inside and outside your home. What is their purpose? Illumination? Protection? Guidance? How does your home shine the light of Christ?

The candles at the altar and on the walls of your church bring light and warmth to prayer. Wax candles sacrifice themselves in order to provide light. How do candles symbolize the mission of your parish?

When do you light candles at home? Birthdays? Meals? How do they bring meaning to events and places?

73. Luke 6:46-49

In the Bible
Jesus wants his disciples to listen to his words and act on them. He compares good disciples to a man who dug deeply and laid the foundation of his new house on rock. It endures the adversity of floods.

In the Liturgy
This is one of the options for the gospel reading when the bishop arrives to bless the site where a new church is to be built (Chapter I). The people gather with him outdoors for the ceremony.

In Your Heart
How strong is the house where you live? Are you grateful for the people who built it? How were they models of the good disciple?

Upon what foundation is your life built? Upon Christ? Upon certain people in the circle of your family and friends? Upon some organization? Is the foundation secure?

Your new church will rise upon physical foundations. Who are the people who have provided the spiritual foundation for your community? Thank God for their witness.

74. Luke 19:1-10

In the Bible
On the road to Jericho, Jesus spots Zacchaeus in a tree. Jesus tells him to hurry down so that he can dine with him. Zacchaeus immediately pledges to right the wrongs he has committed, and Jesus proclaims, "Today salvation has come to this house."

In the Liturgy
This entire passage is one option for the gospel at the dedication of a church (Chapters II and III) and for its anniversary Mass (Chapter VIII).

At the dedication of a church, when the litany of supplication comes to an end, the bishop offers a prayer (Chapter II and III). Just before he dedicates the building, he refers to verse 9 when he prays that it "may be a house of salvation and grace"—like the home of Zacchaeus.

In Your Heart
How has Christ visited your home? Can you recall specific events when you sensed the presence of Christ in a special way? Was anyone there with you?

How is your home a place of salvation? Has Christ saved people through your home? Have you helped others?

Christ comes to your new church to make it his dwelling place. He offers salvation to those who gather there. How is your parish a center of salvation? Who is being saved? From what?

75. John 2:13-22

In the Bible
Jesus entered the temple area and found people selling animals and changing money. He made a whip of cords and drove them out, saying "Stop making my Father's house a marketplace!" Then, speaking of his own body, he said, "Destroy this temple, and in three days I will raise it up."

In the Liturgy
When a bishop dedicates a new church, the liturgy uses a special preface to introduce the eucharistic prayer (Chapter II). Referring to the part of this passage where Jesus compares the temple to his body (verse 21), the bishop praises God the Father, "For you made the Body of your Son . . . the Temple consecrated to you."

At the dedication of the church (Chapters II and III) and on the anniversary of the dedication (Chapter VIII), this is one of the options for the gospel reading at Mass. These passages remind people of the holiness of the place where they worship and the connection between the physical building and Jesus' body.

In Your Heart

How is your parish church maintained as a house of prayer? What activities consecrate it for worship?

How was Jesus' body like the temple in Jerusalem? How is Jesus' body like your parish church? How is your church a sign of resurrection?

How do you experience Christ in your home? How is your home a temple of the Body of Christ? What activities consecrate your home?

76. John 4:19-24

In the Bible

While visiting with Jesus at Jacob's well, a Samaritan woman draws a distinction between her ancestors and his, based on where they worshiped. Jesus tells her that "true worshipers will worship the Father in spirit and truth."

In the Liturgy

At the dedication of a new church, the bishop offers a prayer to conclude the litany of supplication (Chapters II and III). He asks God that this building may become a place "where the Christian people, gathering as one, will worship you in spirit and truth." He wants God to recognize them as the people Jesus foresaw.

When the bishop comes to dedicate a new altar in a previously dedicated church, this is one passage that may serve as the gospel (Chapter IV). At the same Mass, Jesus' response to the woman may supply the verse for the gospel acclamation.

At the dedication of your parish church (Chapters II and III) and on the anniversary of the dedication (Chapter VIII), this is one of the passages that may be proclaimed as the gospel at Mass.

In Your Heart

Where did your ancestors worship? Have you also worshiped there?

What does it mean to worship in spirit and truth? How do you engage your spirit when you pray? How do you keep your prayer true?

The prayers offered at the altar of your church need to be made in spirit and truth. How do you turn your attention to the words of the eucharistic prayer at Mass? Are you praying at your altar in spirit and truth?

77. John 6:35, 48

In the Bible

After the miracle of the loaves, Jesus gives his disciples an important discourse on the bread of life. Twice he declares, "I am the bread of life."

In the Liturgy

When a bishop blesses a new chapel or oratory, the Mass includes a blessing of an altar (Chapter V). He uses the same blessing for a movable altar to be used on different occasions and locations (Chapter VI). In both cases, he refers to the altar as "the table where we break the bread of life."

When a priest blesses a new chalice and paten outside of Mass, the ceremony includes a list of suggested petitions for the universal prayer (Chapter VII). One of these addresses Christ as the Son of God who satisfies our hunger and thirst "by the Bread of life" and the cup of salvation.

In Your Heart

Jesus' teaching was so dramatic that it turned some people away. How do you respond when you hear his words, "I am the bread of life"?

In what ways are you hungering for Christ right now? How does he satisfy you in your prayer? In the Eucharist?

The newly blessed paten will be used to serve the bread of life to the priest and the people of God. How do you prepare yourself for Holy Communion?

78. John 6:54-55

In the Bible
After the miracle of the loaves, Jesus delivers his important discourse on the bread of life to his disciples. At its climax, he proclaims, "Those who eat my flesh and drink my blood have eternal life."

In the Liturgy
When a parish installs a new altar inside a previously dedicated church, the bishop comes to dedicate it (Chapter IV). The preface for that occasion foresees the local fulfillment of Jesus' proclamation when the bishop speaks of the table where God's children are "fed by the Body of Christ."

In Your Heart
Jesus left us his Body and Blood as food and drink. What do you remember from your First Communion? How did you prepare? What did it mean to respond to Jesus' command for the first time?

The new altar in your parish is also the table of communion. It represents the sacrifice of Christ and the sharing of a sacred meal. How do you prepare yourself to feast at this table? How does feeding on the Body of Christ equip you and your community for ministry in the coming week?

In your home, how often do you gather at table with others? What else does this meal accomplish besides physical nourishment? How do you feed on the presence of Christ in your home?

79. John 6:56-57

In the Bible
After the miracle of the loaves, Jesus delivers his discourse on the bread of life. He promises to abide in those who eat his flesh and drink his blood. "Whoever eats me will live because of me."

In the Liturgy
When a priest blesses a new chalice and paten, either of these verses may be sung in the gospel acclamation during the Liturgy of the Word (Chapter VII).

In Your Heart
How does Christ abide with you? How does the receiving of communion fill the people of your parish with the presence of Christ?

The vessels being blessed are set aside for sacred purposes, to be used only for the Eucharist. Do you have special cups and plates at home? When do you use them? What do they mean for you and your family?

What do you think Jesus means when he says that those who eat him live because of him? How has your life been enriched through eating the Body of Christ?

80. John 6:63c

In the Bible
As Jesus concludes his discourse on the bread of life, he tells his disciples, "The words that I have spoken to you are spirit and life." He thus underscored the significance of the teaching that they had just received.

In the Liturgy
At the dedication of a new church, the first reading always comes from Nehemiah, and the responsorial always comes

from Psalm 19 (Chapter II). These passages show the importance of the Word of God to the people of the Old Testament. The antiphon for the responsorial psalm, however, is based on this saying of Jesus from the New Testament. The parish community has just heard the Word of the Lord for the first time from the new ambo. This refrain has the worshipers declare their belief in the power of Jesus' teaching in general, but especially his teaching about the bread of life: "Your words, Lord, are Spirit and life."

In Your Heart
How have the words of Christ given you life? Which of his sayings have especially shaped your beliefs and actions?

How do the words of Christ give you spirit? Do you sense the presence of the Holy Spirit when you hear the Word of the Lord proclaimed in your parish church?

What reverence do you give the Word of the Lord in your home? Where do you keep your Bible? How do you use it? What does that say about the way that the words of Christ give you spirit and life?

81. John 7:37-39

In the Bible
Jesus invites those who believe in him to drink from him. Then he promises that out of the believer's heart will flow rivers of living water. He alludes to passages such as Isaiah 12:3 and Ezekiel 47:1, where the prophets foresaw people drawing water from the springs of salvation and envisioned water flowing freely from the temple. These waters will flow from the one who believes in Jesus.

In the Liturgy

When the bishop dedicates a new altar in a previously dedicated church, the liturgy gives him a special preface to begin the eucharistic prayer (Chapter IV). The bishop declares to God that the newly dedicated altar is the place where "the faithful drink of your Spirit from the streams that flow from Christ."

When the bishop blesses a new altar in a new chapel or oratory, he prays that "it be the fountain from which flows an unending stream of salvation" (Chapter V). He uses the same prayer when blessing a movable altar or a new one in a previously blessed chapel (Chapter VI).

In Your Heart

How do you drink from Christ? When do you most listen to his words? When do you most sense his presence?

How do others drink from Christ within you? How does Christ use you as one stream of his fountain of salvation?

How is your faith community a river of living water? Besides common prayer, what activities make it clear that you all bring life to a thirsty world?

82. John 11:51-52

In the Bible

Shortly before the arrest of Jesus, Caiaphas counseled that it was better to have one man die for the people than to have the whole nation destroyed. John comments that he spoke this as a prophecy for the meaning of the death of Jesus, which would "gather into one the dispersed children of God."

In the Liturgy

At the end of the Mass of dedication or of the blessing of a church, the bishop offers a solemn blessing (Chapters II, III, and V). He recalls that God "has willed that all his scattered children be gathered in his Son." The same blessing occurs at the end of the Mass on the anniversary of the dedication (Chapter VIII).

When the bishop comes to dedicate a new altar in a previously dedicated church, he offers a special preface to begin the eucharistic prayer (Chapter IV). He declares that the altar is the place where God's children "are gathered into the one holy Church." As the cross of Christ gathered God's dispersed children, so does this altar.

In Your Heart
The altar of your parish church gathers people who are scattered. Some have traveled some distance to come. Some you may not even know. As you think about your parish community at the altar, why have they come here? What do they share in common? How has the death of Christ gathered them?

Who is missing from your table at church or at home? How would you describe your feelings about them? Are they longing to be gathered together with you?

The altar in your parish church is a point of gathering, but that requires a previous invitation. How does your parish community invite nonbelievers to gather at this altar? How do you introduce others to Christ? Whom might you introduce to the community that gathers at your parish altar?

83. John 12:31-36a

In the Bible
In one of the final discourses before his arrest, Jesus indicates the kind of death he will undergo: "I, when I am lifted up from the earth, will draw all people to myself." He urges his followers to walk in his light while he is among them so that they may become children of the light.

In the Liturgy

When a new altar is being dedicated in a previously dedicated church, this is one of the passages that may be proclaimed as the gospel in the Liturgy of the Word (Chapter IV). It connects the images of cross and light to this new altar, near which will stand a crucifix and candles.

In the collect of the same Mass, the bishop prays to God, "who willed to draw all things to your Son, lifted high on the altar of the Cross."

In Your Heart

How has the cross drawn you to Christ? How has his sacrifice inspired you? Has it saved you? From what?

Whenever the priest incenses the altar at Mass, he also incenses the cross, drawing these two symbols into a relationship. The altar becomes the place where you encounter the death and resurrection of Christ. How does the altar in your church resemble the cross, drawing people to Christ?

Jesus wanted his followers to become children of the light. When you see the candles lighted at the altar of your church, how do they represent Christ to you? How do they challenge you? How are you to become the bright light of Christ?

84. John 15:5

In the Bible

At the Last Supper, Jesus assures his disciples that he is the vine, and they are the branches. They will bear much fruit if they abide in him.

In the Liturgy

When the bishop dedicates a church, a centerpiece of the celebration is the lengthy and eloquent prayer of dedication

(Chapters II and III). In it he refers not only to the church as the building, but to the church as the people, "the chosen vine of the Lord, whose branches fill the whole world, and whose tendrils, borne on the wood of the Cross, reach upward to the Kingdom of Heaven."

In Your Heart
How are you a branch on the vine of Christ? How do you feel connected to Christ? What connects you to others on the same vine?

Jesus lived in a part of the world where vines are common. What plants are common where you live? How do they represent the life of Christ to you?

Your new parish church will celebrate the branches that make up the community. What holds your parish together as branches on the vine? Besides the celebration of the Mass, what other activities connect people? How do you participate in these?

85. John 19:34

In the Bible
At the crucifixion, one of the soldiers pierced Jesus' side with a spear. Blood and water poured forth from the wound.

In the Liturgy
When the bishop dedicates a new altar in a previously dedicated church, he offers an eloquent prayer of dedication (Chapter IV). During it, he prays that the altar may be a sign of Christ, "from whose pierced side flowed blood and water, by which were established the Sacraments of the Church." The Eucharist and baptism are represented in John's account of the pierced side of Christ, who even in death gives life.

In Your Heart
Almost every image of the crucifixion depicts the wounded side
of Christ. Meditate on that moment when blood and water
flowed out. Even in his death, how has Christ offered you life?

Your parish community will be a place where people celebrate the sacraments of the church. How do you prepare people
for baptism and communion? How does preparation for the
sacraments connect to this altar and to the cross?

How do you offer your life to others? How do people encounter the sacraments of the church through you?

86. Acts 2:42-47

In the Bible
Following Pentecost, when the disciples received the gift of the
Holy Spirit, they lived together in unity. They devoted themselves to teaching, breaking bread, and prayers. They held all
things in common. They prayed at the temple and broke bread
in their homes. The Lord increased their number day by day.

In the Liturgy
This is one of the passages that may be read at the dedication
of a new altar in a previously dedicated church (Chapter IV). If
the ceremony takes place during the fifty days of Easter Time,
this may serve as the first reading.

In Your Heart
What are your happiest memories of sharing Christianity?
When have you felt most united with other people in your
parish, whether in prayer, possessions, or service?

The Lord increased the number of believers as people witnessed the life of the first disciples. How are people hearing
about your parish community? How do you personally invite
others to experience life at your new altar?

The altar in your parish church will provide a place where you will gather in common prayer with others who share your faith. When else do you see those people? Where? What do you do in common?

87. Acts 4:8-12

In the Bible
While Peter was under arrest for preaching about Christ, he boldly preached to those who had apprehended him. He cited the verse from Psalm 118 about the stone rejected by the builders that had become the cornerstone. The stone is Jesus, and the guilty builders are the people who had supervised his death and who had just arrested Peter.

In the Liturgy
As the bishop blesses the site for a new church building, the parish community gathers for prayer (Chapter I). This is one of the passages that may be proclaimed as the first reading. It reassures the people that Christ, the cornerstone of their faith, will be the rock of this building.

In Your Heart
How has Jesus Christ become the cornerstone of your faith? Have you felt that all your life? Or was there a moment when this became clear to you?

Jesus was rejected by the authorities but rose from the dead to affirm people's faith in him. Has your parish community gone through a difficult time to arrive at its day of dedication? Looking back on it, how has Christ been the rock of strength?

This new church will be the place where your community gathers for worship. How else does your parish live out its belief that Christ is the cornerstone?

88. Acts 7:44-50

In the Bible
After his arrest and just before his martyrdom, Stephen gives a brief history of the houses of God: Moses's tent of testimony in the desert and Solomon's temple in Jerusalem. Stephen then cites Isaiah 66:1-2, in order to show that the Lord does not require an earthly building. He sees a vision of Jesus within God's dwelling place in the heavens, essentially inviting his listeners to find in Christ the fulfillment of their temple.

In the Liturgy
At the dedication of a church already in use (Chapter III) or on the anniversary celebration of the dedication of a parish church (Chapter VIII), this passage may be proclaimed as the first reading during Easter Time.

In Your Heart
The people of Israel prayed in different places before the construction of Solomon's temple. What do you know of the history of your parish church? Where did people pray before the present building opened? What does that tell you about the presence of God in your community?

During Easter Time, we hear many readings from Acts of the Apostles. Stephen testified bravely to his belief in the risen Christ. How does Easter resound in your heart? How do others learn about your faith in the risen Christ?

God dwells in the heavens and does not need buildings. Your parish church has been a place where you encounter God in prayer. Where else have you experienced the presence of God?

89. Romans 4:9, 11

In the Bible
Paul explains how both Jews and Gentiles are children of Abraham. Abraham received the gift of faith before he was circumcised. Therefore, even those outside the original covenant may be brought into the family of God—if they have faith.

In the Liturgy
When the bishop dedicates a new altar in a previously dedicated church, he offers a special prayer of dedication (Chapter IV). He speaks about some of the Old Testament figures who had constructed altars, including Noah and Abraham, whom he calls "our father in faith."

In Your Heart
Who are the people who gave birth to your faith? Were they your parents, or did someone else do this for you?

Reflect on the story of Abraham. How is his response to God's call an inspiration to you? What is the hardest thing you've done as an act of your faith and trust in God?

The new altar in your church will be the central place for celebrating the Mass. How do the people who gather there show that they are children of Abraham? How does your parish community come in faith to show their trust in God?

90. Romans 6:3-7, 11

In the Bible
Paul tells the Romans that they were baptized into the death of Christ. As they were buried with him by baptism into his death, so they will walk in newness of life. They are dead to sin and alive to God in Christ Jesus.

In the Liturgy

When the bishop dedicates a new church or an altar, he leads a sprinkling rite at the beginning (Chapters II, III, and IV). One of its purposes is to remind the gathered community that they were baptized in Christ. As he blesses the water, he prays to God, who established "that those who descend as sinners into the sacred waters to die with Christ should rise free from guilt."

In the same ceremonies, when the bishop dedicates the new church building, he prays, "Here may the flood of divine grace overwhelm human offenses, so that your children, Father, being dead to sin, may be reborn to heavenly life."

In Your Heart

When were you baptized? What do you remember of it? Or, if you were too young at the time, what have you heard about the day of your baptism? Who are your godparents? How have they helped you rise with Christ?

Baptism lets us rise to walk in newness of life. How does your baptism still influence your life? How does it provide you hope? When you sign yourself with holy water or participate in the sprinkling of blessed water at church, how does it affect you?

We all repeatedly recommit ourselves to Christ and to our baptism. How do you still need to die to sin? How are you alive for God in Christ Jesus?

91. Romans 12:1

In the Bible

Paul appeals to the Romans to present their very bodies as a living sacrifice, holy and acceptable to God. They do not offer sacrifices from their crops and herds, but from their very lives.

In the Liturgy

The offering of ourselves as a living sacrifice is foundational to the eucharistic prayer at any Mass. As we join in the offering of the Body and Blood of Christ, so we offer our very lives to the Father.

When the bishop dedicates a new church, the ceremony includes an incensation of the altar and the walls of the building (Chapters II and III). The introduction to this ceremony, citing this passage from Romans, explains, "the People of God are incensed first, for they are the living temple in which each faithful member is a spiritual altar."

When the bishop blesses an altar for a new chapel or for occasional usage, he offers a special prayer (Chapters V and VI). He prays that the gathered community may grow into a holy temple "and offer on the altar of our heart the sacrifice of a life spent in holiness, pleasing and acceptable" to the praise of God's glory.

At the Mass celebrating the anniversary of the dedication of your parish church (Chapter VIII), the priest makes this petition in the prayer over the offerings: "we pray that you may make of us a sacrificial offering always acceptable to you."

In Your Heart

In what ways do you offer your life to God? In your family, at school, or at work, how does God receive a pleasing sacrifice from you?

Christ gave us a model of sacrifice. His life was completely lived for the Father. Who else has given you an example of sacrifice? How do those people still inspire you?

Your parish community celebrates the sacrifice of Christ at every Mass. How does your parish sacrifice for others? What activities or events do you think make a pleasing sacrifice to God?

92. 1 Corinthians 3:9c-11, 16-17

In the Bible

Paul explains the role that the Corinthians play in service to the Gospel. They are God's building. They are also coworkers who build up God's dwelling place upon the foundation of Jesus Christ. They are the temple of God, and God's Spirit dwells within them.

In the Liturgy

The commentary on the blessing of a site for the construction of a new church recalls that the structure will be a visible sign of the living Church, "God's building," which the faithful constitute (Chapter I). Verse 9c is the very first biblical reference in the entire collection of ceremonies pertaining to the dedication of a church. It shows the centrality of the people whom the building represents.

In the same ceremony, during the readings from Scripture, the people may sing verses from Psalm 118, along with a refrain inspired by 1 Corinthians 3:11, "There is no foundation other than Jesus Christ." When the bishop blesses the cornerstone, he recalls that the apostle Paul called Jesus "the sure and firm foundation."

When the new church is dedicated, the bishop sprinkles the people, the altar, and the walls with blessed water (Chapters II and III). When he finishes, he alludes to verse 16 when he prays, "May God, the Father of mercies, by the grace of the Holy Spirit, cleanse us who are the temple where he dwells."

In the same ceremonies, the entire passage may be proclaimed as one of the readings at the Mass. When the bishop and priests anoint the altar and the walls, along with Psalm 84, the people may sing a refrain inspired by verse 9c: "Holy is the temple of the Lord, God's own structure, God's own building."

At the conclusion of the dedication or blessing of a church, the bishop offers a solemn blessing over the people (Chapters

II, III, and V). Alluding to verse 16, he prays that they may become God's "temple and the dwelling place of the Holy Spirit."
The same blessing occurs at the end of the Mass on the anniversary of the dedication (Chapter VIII).

When the bishop dedicates a church that is already in use
(Chapter III), he offers the same preface that introduces the
eucharistic prayer at the anniversary of the dedication of the
church (Chapter VIII), with its declaration, "Here you build
up for yourself the temple that we are."

This entire passage may be proclaimed as one of the readings
at the anniversary celebration of the dedication of your parish
church (Chapter VIII). In the same ceremony, the communion
antiphon is based on verses 16-17: "You are the temple of God,
and the Spirit of God dwells in you. The temple of God, which
you are, is holy."

In Your Heart
You are God's building. How have you experienced the presence of God's Holy Spirit dwelling within you?

Even though your parish church is the structure where you
encounter God together with others, your entire parish is a living temple of God. Which members of your parish community
especially signify God's dwelling place to you? Why?

You are God's temple built on the foundation of Jesus Christ.
How is Christ the foundation of your life? What recent decisions have you made because you value Christian principles?

93. 1 Corinthians 6:19

In the Bible
St. Paul appeals to the Corinthians to act in a morally upright
way. He reminds them who they are: "Do you not know that
your body is a temple of the Holy Spirit within you, which you
have from God, and that you are not your own?"

In the Liturgy

Near the beginning of the ceremony when a bishop dedicates a new church or altar, he blesses water for sprinkling on the people, the altar, and the walls (Chapters II, III, and IV). He asks God that the water may be a sign of the baptismal waters, "in which we have been washed in Christ and made a temple of your Spirit."

If the church being dedicated has already been in use by the faithful, the bishop offers a special preface to introduce the eucharistic prayer (Chapter III). He praises God because "Here you build up for yourself the temple that we are." The same preface is used at the anniversary Mass for the dedication of a church (Chapter VIII).

In Your Heart

How have you experienced that your body is a temple of the Holy Spirit dwelling within you? What wonders have you witnessed? How have you felt God's presence?

How do you use your body in ways that build up the body of Christ, the church? How has your physical activity shared the spiritual reality of your faith?

Your parish church is a place where God builds up the temple that is the body of believers. How has your parish demonstrated the presence of the Holy Spirit among its members?

94. 1 Corinthians 10:1-6

In the Bible

St. Paul interprets an episode from Israel's exodus from Egypt. All were "baptized" with Moses in the cloud and the sea, all ate the same spiritual food, and all drank from the spiritual rock. Then Paul writes, astonishingly, "and the rock was Christ."

In the Liturgy
This is one of the passages that may be read when people gather with their bishop for the blessing of the building site (Chapter I). As the construction of a new church begins, a cornerstone may be laid, and the people hear about Christ the rock.

The bishop refers to this passage in the preface of the Mass where he dedicates an altar in a previously dedicated church (Chapter IV). He proclaims to God, "Here the faithful drink of your Spirit from the streams that flow from Christ, the spiritual rock."

In Your Heart
How has Christ been the rock of your life? What occasions can you recall when you "drank from the streams" that came from the spiritual rock that is Christ?

How is the altar in your parish church a source of streams for drinking? Apart from the Blood of Christ consecrated on this altar, how has Christ given you drink through your participation at the Mass?

How is Christ the rock of your parish community? How have you witnessed the impact of his teaching among the people with whom you worship?

95. 1 Corinthians 10:14-22a

In the Bible
St. Paul urges the Corinthians to turn away from false worship and to eat and drink only the Body and Blood of Christ. He focuses on the vessel: "The cup of blessing that we bless, is it not a sharing in the blood of Christ?" The many become one by sharing in the one bread.

In the Liturgy

When the bishop dedicates an altar in a previously dedicated church, the second reading may come from verses 16-21 of this passage (Chapter IV). The introduction to the same ceremony uses verses 16-17 to explain the purpose of the altar, the place where the cup is shared and the bread is broken, the Body and Blood of Christ that bring the many into one.

When a priest blesses a new chalice and paten, verses 14-22a form one of the passages that may be read at the ceremony (Chapter VII).

In Your Heart

At Mass, how have you experienced the unity of the Body of Christ at communion? You probably feel at one with Christ. Do you also feel at one with those who receive communion with you?

What does it mean to share in the Blood of Christ? He poured out his Blood for the salvation of others. How do you pour yourself out for other people? Do you donate blood? Who are the ones who most benefit from your service?

What have you noticed about the sacred vessels at your church? How are they made? Where are they stored? How do they inspire your faith in the Eucharist?

96. 1 Corinthians 11:23-28

In the Bible

St. Paul passes on to the Corinthians the teaching he has received about Jesus' actions at the Last Supper. Taking a loaf of bread, Jesus said, "This is my body that is for you." Taking a cup, he said, "This cup is the new covenant in my blood." He commanded his disciples, "Do this in remembrance of me."

In the Liturgy

This is one of the passages that contribute to the words that the priest says at the consecration of every Mass. The bishop makes an extra reference to it when he dedicates an altar in a previously dedicated church (Chapter IV). He says in the preface that Christ "has taught us to celebrate for ever the memorial of the Sacrifice."

When a priest blesses a new chalice and paten for use at the Mass, this is one of the passages that may be proclaimed among the readings from scripture (Chapter VII).

In Your Heart

You hear the words of Jesus at every Mass. You participate in the same practice instituted at the Last Supper and handed on by St. Paul. How did you first learn about the Last Supper? Who were the people who handed the teaching on to you?

The Eucharist has formed a part of your life. How do you speak about its importance? Have you shared your faith with others? How have they responded?

Bread is broken, and wine is poured out. How do these actions represent the end of Jesus' life to you? When have you recently broken and poured out yourself for the sake of others? Would you do it again?

97. 1 Corinthians 15:28

In the Bible

As St. Paul writes about the second coming of Christ, he proclaims that all will become subject to God, "so that God may be all in all."

In the Liturgy

When the bishop dedicates a new church, he offers a special preface to introduce the eucharistic prayer (Chapter II). He praises God for making the church the holy city of his eternal presence, "where for endless ages you will be all in all."

In Your Heart
How have you placed yourself subject to Christ and subject to God? What decisions have you made recently that showed you want only what God desires? How does the presence of God within you contribute to the day when God will be all in all?

How is your parish community subject to Christ and subject to God? How have you seen Christian principles at work in the people with whom you worship?

Who are the people who have truly inspired you to follow in their footsteps? How do you choose to subject yourself to their example?

98. 2 Corinthians 2:14-15

In the Bible
St. Paul compares following Christ to spreading the fragrance that comes from knowing him. He tells the Corinthians, "we are the aroma of Christ to God."

In the Liturgy
As the bishop prepares to incense the newly dedicated altar and church for the first time, he offers a prayer that refers to this passage (Chapters II and III): "let your Church be fragrant with the aroma of Christ." He offers the same prayer when dedicating an altar in a previously dedicated church (Chapter IV).

In Your Heart
What are your favorite aromas? What events or people do they call to mind?

Who are the people in your parish whom you consider "fragrant with the aroma of Christ"? When you are in the room with them, how can you tell that they are Christians?

How are you the aroma of Christ to God? How do people detect that you follow Christ?

99. 2 Corinthians 6:16

In the Bible
St. Paul urges the Corinthians to keep their distance from those who practice false worship, especially those who worship false idols in temples. He reminds his readers, "we are the temple of the living God."

In the Liturgy
When the bishop dedicates a church that has already been in use, he offers a special preface at the beginning of the eucharistic prayer (Chapter III). He proclaims to God, "Here you build up for yourself the temple that we are." The same preface is used for the Mass on the occasion of an anniversary celebration of your church's dedication (Chapter VIII).

In Your Heart
What are the primary places where you spend your time? In what way are these "temples"? Are they supporting your worship at church? Or do they compete with it?

The Christian community is a temple of God, represented by the structure that is the church. What parallels do you see between your church building and the people who worship there? How does the building influence the people? How does it represent the people?

Because of your baptism, you are a temple of the living God. At which moments are you particularly aware of God dwelling within you?

100. Ephesians 2:19-22

In the Bible

Addressing Gentile converts, St. Paul asserts that they are full members of the church, no less than the Jewish converts to Christ. He calls them "members of the household of God, built upon the foundation of the apostles and prophets, with Christ Jesus himself as the cornerstone." The whole structure is joined together in Christ and grows into a holy temple, the dwelling place of God.

In the Liturgy

At the commencement of the building project for the new church, the ceremony of blessing makes several allusions to this passage (Chapter I). When the bishop offers his first prayer at the location, he praises God, who established the church "upon the foundation of the Apostles with Christ Jesus himself as chief cornerstone."

The bishop introduces the petitions that conclude the same ceremony by inviting the community to pray that God will make them "the living temple of his glory, built upon the cornerstone of Christ his Son." One of the suggested petitions prays that those who sadly cannot build churches may "build themselves into a living temple." The bishop concludes the petitions asking that all "may grow into the temple" of God's glory.

The bishop returns to dedicate the new church and altar (Chapters II and III). This entire passage may be one of readings for the Mass. When he offers the prayer of dedication, he proclaims that the church is blessed, "standing upon the foundation of the Apostles with Christ Jesus its chief cornerstone."

Another allusion appears in the preface that the bishop offers in the blessing of a newly built church (Chapter II). He prays to God, "You also established the Church as a holy city, built upon the foundation of the Apostles, with Christ Jesus himself the chief cornerstone."

This entire passage may be used as one of the readings at the Mass that celebrates the anniversary of the dedication of your parish church (Chapter VIII).

In Your Heart
The foundation of your faith goes back to the time of the apostles and prophets. What gospel passages come to mind when you think about the faith of the apostles? How do those accounts inspire you?

As you think about your parish and the milestones it has passed, who are the people who helped lay the foundation? How does the history of your parish still shape the people who worship there today?

How do you put yourself at the service of others in the church? How do you join the apostles and prophets laying a foundation upon which others may build and grow?

101. Ephesians 3:4

In the Bible
St. Paul expresses that his mission is to help people perceive his understanding of the mystery of Christ.

In the Liturgy
During the dedication of a new church, the bishop begins the eucharistic prayer with a special preface (Chapter II). He praises God for allowing us to consecrate "apt places for the divine mysteries."

In Your Heart

How did you come to understand the mystery of Christ? Who first shared Christ with you?

What aspects of faith are especially full of mystery for you? How does Christ give you hope?

Whenever you return to this church, you may encounter the mystery of Christ through the Eucharist. Where else do you experience the mystery of Christ? How does your parish church provide a home for your faith and wonder?

102. Ephesians 4:2

In the Bible

St. Paul urges the Ephesians to be worthy of their calling and to love one another with humility, gentleness, and patience.

In the Liturgy

When the bishop dedicates a new church, he introduces and concludes the appeal to the saints in the litany of supplication (Chapters II and III). In his closing prayer, he asks that the new church may be a house of salvation and grace where the Christian people will "be built up in charity."

In Your Heart

The dedication of your new parish church is also a rededication of your parish community. How have the preparations for this day built everyone up in charity?

How have you experienced the love of God through the members of your parish church? How will the new church building foster that spirit of charity?

Where can you bring more charity to your community? How do you usually build others up, to make them worthy of their calling as followers of Christ?

103. Ephesians 4:15-16

In the Bible
St. Paul speaks about the duty of the body of Christ to grow up in every way into Christ, the head. In this way the whole body promotes the body's growth, building itself up in love.

In the Liturgy
When the bishop dedicates a church that has already been in use, he offers a special preface (Chapter III). He declares that in this church God builds up the members "to grow ever more and more as the Lord's own Body." The same preface is used at the Mass for the anniversary of the dedication of the church (Chapter VIII).

In Your Heart
Even as your parish church grows older, it continually builds up its members in love. In your years of association with this parish, how have you seen it grow in faith?

You are a member of the Body of Christ, and you have Christ as your head. How does Christ entrust part of his mission to you? How do you build up the body of Christ in love?

What does it mean to have Christ as your head? To whom else do you turn for leadership in your life? How do you seek guidance from them and from Christ?

104. Ephesians 5:2

In the Bible
St. Paul urges the Ephesians to live in love as Christ loved us and gave himself up as a fragrant offering and sacrifice to God.

In the Liturgy
When the bishop dedicates a new altar in a previously dedicated church, he introduces the eucharistic prayer with a special

preface (Chapter IV). There he recalls that Christ "taught us to celebrate for ever the memorial of the Sacrifice that he himself offered to you on the altar of the Cross." In this place, "the Sacrifice of Christ is ever offered in mystery."

In Your Heart
St. Paul says that Christ offered himself to the Father out of love, and he urges us to love in the same way. How do you express your love? How does it feel when you sacrifice for someone you love? Do you feel resentful or fulfilled?

In what ways did Christ offer himself to the Father? How do you imitate Christ in your life?

At the Mass you will be entering the mystery of the sacrifice of Christ at a new altar. When you participate at Mass, how do you unite your own sacrifices with the sacrifice of Christ at the altar of your parish church?

105. Colossians 2:9

In the Bible
Exploring the mystery of faith for his readers, St. Paul declares that the whole fullness of God dwells bodily in Christ.

In the Liturgy
When the bishop dedicates a new church, he uses a special preface to introduce the eucharistic prayer (Chapter II). He calls Christ "the Temple consecrated to you, in which the fullness of the Godhead might dwell."

In Your Heart
We proclaim that Christ is the Son of God, fully God and fully human. How do you imagine Christ when you pray?

The gospels are filled with episodes that affirm the divinity of Christ. Which are your favorites? Why?

As the fullness of the Godhead dwelled in Jesus Christ, so Christ comes to dwell in your new church. When you enter a church building, how do you most sense the presence of Christ? In the design? The decoration? The people?

106. Colossians 3:14

In the Bible
St. Paul advises the Colossians how to live by describing virtues as articles of clothing. Above all he admonishes them, "clothe yourselves with love, which binds everything together in perfect harmony."

In the Liturgy
When the bishop dedicates a new church, he uses a special preface to introduce the eucharistic prayer (Chapter II). He praises God for establishing the church as a holy city "given life by the Spirit and bonded by charity."

In Your Heart
How is your parish community like a city? What binds the people together? What services do they receive? How do they support one another?

You practice many virtues. How does love bind them all together in your life? When you make difficult decisions, how do you let love guide the answers?

Your new church is to be the place where your parish is formed as a community in Christ. How does love already bind the people of your parish? How have you witnessed love in action among the members?

107. Hebrews 4:14; 5:5-6

In the Bible
In several places, the letter to the Hebrews assigns Christ the title of priest. He is the great, sinless high priest who has entered the heavens (4:14). He is the fulfillment of the prophecy about Melchizedek, a priest forever (5:5-6).

In the Liturgy
When the bishop dedicates a new altar for a previously dedicated church, he offers a special preface to introduce the eucharistic prayer (Chapter IV). Near the beginning, he praises God for Christ, who became "both the true Priest and the true oblation."

In Your Heart
The priests of the Old Testament offered sacrifice to God. How is Christ the fulfillment of their ministry? How do the priests of your parish imitate Christ the priest?

You were baptized into the priesthood of Jesus Christ. How does Christ the priest act through you and other members of your parish?

What is the hardest sacrifice you have made? Whom did it benefit? Do you believe it pleased God?

108. Hebrews 12:18-19, 22-24

In the Bible
The letter to the Hebrews explains worship as drawing near to "the city of the living God, the heavenly Jerusalem, and to innumerable angels in festal gathering . . . and to Jesus, the mediator of a new covenant." Worship today foreshadows life in heaven.

In the Liturgy

Before construction begins on a new church, the bishop goes to bless the site (Chapter I). In his first prayer, he asks God that the people may grow into the temple of his glory until "they come at last to the heavenly city."

When the bishop returns to dedicate the new church, he blesses water and sprinkles it upon the people, the walls, and the altar (Chapters II and III). He prays that all who celebrate the divine mysteries in this church "may come at last to the heavenly Jerusalem." He does the same at the dedication of an altar in a previously dedicated church (Chapter IV).

At the dedication of the church, this passage is one option for the second reading (Chapters II and III). In the prayer of dedication within the same ceremonies, the bishop says, "Here may the joyful offering of praise resound, with human voices joined to the song of Angels" and that all may "come exultant to the Jerusalem which is above."

If the bishop is dedicating a church that has already been in use, he offers the appropriate preface (Chapter III). He thanks God for building up the people into a temple that grows ever more as the Lord's Body, "till she reaches her fullness in the vision of peace, the heavenly city of Jerusalem." A priest will offer the same preface when the parish celebrates its anniversaries of this dedication (Chapter VIII).

This entire passage may be proclaimed as one of the readings at Mass for the anniversary of a parish church (Chapter VIII).

In Your Heart

Both the building that is the church and the people who are the church foreshadow heaven. What aspects of your church building transport you to a participation in the life to come?

How have you anticipated the happiness of heaven through the people of your parish? How do their voices and actions join with those of the angels?

What are your favorite images of heaven? How would it be like a peaceful city? How have you already experienced a peaceful city in your life?

109. Hebrews 13:8-15

In the Bible
The letter to the Hebrews admonishes Christians not to be carried away by strange teachings. It compares Jesus' suffering to the shedding of blood in the animal sacrifices of the old covenant. "For here we have no lasting city, but we are looking for the city that is to come." We offer a sacrifice of praise to God.

In the Liturgy
This passage may be proclaimed as one of the readings at the dedication of an altar in a previously dedicated church (Chapter IV). Its opening verse may accompany the gospel acclamation of the same celebration.

In Your Heart
Some people have given their lives for the sake of others. Which of them have touched you the most? People from your family? Historical figures? Why?

Jesus Christ is the same yesterday, today and forever. What "strange teachings" have you avoided? How does your faith in Christ hold you steady?

The new altar of your parish church will be the center for the sacrifice of the Mass. You will witness the consecration of the Blood of Christ. Christ invites his disciples to drink the Blood he poured out for them. How has your communion in Christ helped you sacrifice for others?

110. James 2:1

In the Bible
St. James challenges his readers to show that they "really believe" in Jesus Christ by avoiding acts of favoritism.

In the Liturgy
When the bishop blesses the site of a new church at the start of its construction, he may help lay the cornerstone (Chapter I). He does this "in the faith of Jesus Christ," in hopes that this new church may offer the strength and grace of the sacraments to all.

In Your Heart
How has your parish community avoided acts of favoritism? How does it practice an open door to all?

In your own life, how do your deeds show your faith in Jesus Christ? How have you shown you "really believe"?

As your new church is being built, how can you help all others find a home in it? Which organizations in your parish are best suited to share faith in Jesus Christ? How does your parish mission statement commit to the teachings of Jesus?

111. 1 Peter 2:4-9

In the Bible
St. Peter invites new Christians to come to Christ, the living stone, rejected by mortals, yet chosen by God. They themselves are to be living stones, built into a spiritual house. He quotes several passages from the Old Testament: Isaiah 28:16; Psalm 118:22; and Isaiah 8:14.

In the Liturgy
At the blessing of the construction site for a new church, the suggested universal prayer refers to this passage several times

(Chapter I). The bishop invites the people to pray that God "will be pleased to make them into the living temple of his glory." Among the suggested petitions, one asks that all those prevented from building churches "may strive to build themselves into a living temple," while another prays that "all here present, as living stones," may be found worthy of the divine mysteries to be celebrated there. The bishop concludes these petitions asking that all "may grow into the temple" of God's glory.

When the bishop returns to dedicate the new church (Chapter II), he invites the people to pray that they "may grow into a spiritual temple." In the Liturgy of the Word for a church dedication, this passage may serve as the second reading (Chapters II and III). In the same ceremonies, when the bishop begins the litany of supplication, he invites all to pray to God "who makes the hearts of the faithful into spiritual temples for himself." In the prayer of dedication, he declares that the Church is "a holy temple built of living stones." In the preface for the dedication of a new building (Chapter II), he calls the church "a city to be built of chosen stones."

When a previously dedicated church receives a new altar, the bishop uses a special preface to introduce the eucharistic prayer (Chapter IV). He praises God for the new altar, where, through Christ, "they, too, become a holy oblation, a living altar."

When the bishop blesses an altar for a chapel or one that may be transported to different sites, the prayer that he offers refers to this passage (Chapters V and VI). He asks God that "as we come to Christ, the living stone, we may grow in him into a holy temple."

The entire passage may be proclaimed as one of the readings at the Mass for the anniversary of the dedication of the parish church (Chapter VIII).

In Your Heart
How is Christ the living stone in your life? How has your reliance on Christ developed over the years?

How are the people of your parish like living stones? How have you seen them join together in faith? When have you joined in these activities?

Your church and altar are signs of the community. If the altar especially represents Christ, how do the walls represent the people of the church? How is your church built of living stones that have a dynamic impact on the surrounding community? How do you form a strong wall of faith?

112. Revelation 1:6

In the Bible
John writes to the seven churches of Asia. He begins with an acclamation of Jesus Christ: "to him be glory and dominion forever and ever. Amen."

In the Liturgy
The bishop may bless the cornerstone to be laid at the commencement of construction of a new church (Chapter I). As he lays the first stone, he praises Jesus Christ, the cornerstone of our faith: "To him be glory and power for all the ages of eternity."

In Your Heart
The community hopes that the church under construction will endure for many generations to come. When you look into the future of your parish, how do you see its members giving glory to Christ for all the ages of eternity?

You have received your faith from others. How far back can you trace the ancestry of your faith? Who made a steadfast commitment to praising the glory of Christ?

How have you experienced the power of Christ in your life? How has that same power existed in your family in the past?

113. Revelation 3:12

In the Bible
John writes to the angel of the church in the ancient Turkish city of Philadelphia. Christ promises to make the people there a pillar in the temple of God, writing on them the name of the new city of Jerusalem that comes down from heaven.

In the Liturgy
When the bishop dedicates a church that is already in use, he offers a special preface to introduce the eucharistic prayer (Chapter III). He prays for the community that hopes to reach its fullness "in the vision of peace, the heavenly city of Jerusalem." A priest uses the same preface at the Mass celebrating the anniversary of a church's dedication (Chapter VIII).

In Your Heart
How do you experience peace in the place where you live? What makes you feel secure? How is it a little bit of heaven?

How is your parish church an expression of the new Jerusalem? When you enter the building, how does it help you anticipate entering the joy of heaven?

What are the strengths of your parish community? How are you and other parishioners a pillar in the temple of God?

114. Revelation 5:6

In the Bible
In his vision of heaven, John sees a lamb standing, even though it had been slaughtered. It is an image of Christ, the passover Lamb of God.

In the Liturgy

When a new altar has been built for a previously dedicated church, the bishop offers a special prayer (Chapter IV). He recalls how the altar that Moses built, "sprinkled with the blood of a lamb, would mystically prefigure the altar of the Cross."

In Your Heart

The image of the lamb, slaughtered yet standing, is popular in Christian art. Do you recall seeing a representation of it somewhere in stained glass, paint, or some other medium? How does this image speak to you of Jesus Christ?

Can you think of some people who were wounded and yet are standing? What happened to them? How do they inspire you?

How has Christ helped you overcome your afflictions so that you may stand with him? How has he strengthened your parish community when things looked difficult?

115. Revelation 6:9

In the Bible

In his vision, John beholds an altar. Beneath it are the souls of those slaughtered for the Word of God and for their testimony.

In the Liturgy

This passage supplies a biblical foundation for the practice of placing the relics of saints, especially of martyrs, beneath the altars of Catholic churches. Such relics are not required, but the custom is honored. When a bishop places relics beneath a new altar (Chapters II, III, and IV), all may sing this antiphon: "Beneath the altar of God you have been placed, O saints of God: intercede for us before the Lord Jesus Christ."

In Your Heart

Who are some of the saints who have inspired you? Why?

Who are the most faith-filled people you have come to know in your life? What testimony to Christ have they given? How do you honor their memory? Are they like saints for you?

Are there relics of saints in the altar of your parish church? Who are they? What do you know of their lives? How might their testimony help the specific mission of your parish?

116. Revelation 8:3-4

In the Bible
John sees an angel with a golden censer approach the golden altar before the throne of God in heaven. A great quantity of incense rises with the prayers of all the saints.

In the Liturgy
After the bishop offers the prayer of dedication for a new altar, he incenses it (Chapters II, III, and IV). One antiphon the people may sing is, "An Angel stood by the altar of the Temple holding in his hand a golden censer." Or they may sing, "In the presence of the Lord arose clouds of incense from the hand of the Angel."

This passage may be proclaimed as one of the readings at the Mass of the dedication of a new altar (Chapter IV).

It may be used as the offertory antiphon for the anniversary Mass of the dedication of the parish church (Chapter VIII).

In Your Heart
What are your thoughts when you see smoke arising from incense at church? What do you notice about its patterns? How does it imitate your prayer?

Where else do you regularly see rising smoke? What does it signify? How do you respond when you see it?

At the dedication of the new altar in your parish church, which of your prayers will you send like smoke? If you could have God's full attention for a few minutes, what would you most want to say? Would they be words of praise? Repentance? Petition?

117. Revelation 21:1-5a

In the Bible
John sees a new heaven and a new earth. The new Jerusalem comes down from heaven like a bride adorned. In a proclamation reminiscent of Ezekiel 37:27, a voice declares that God makes his home among mortals. Verse 10 of the same chapter 21 also refers to John's vision of the holy city.

In the Liturgy
When the bishop arrives to bless the site of a church about to be built (Chapter I), he prays that all the people may grow into the temple of God's glory until "they come at last to the heavenly city."

The bishop blesses water near the beginning of the celebration of the dedication of a new church or altar (Chapters II, III, and IV). He prays that those "who will celebrate the divine mysteries. . . may come at last to the heavenly Jerusalem."

At the dedication of a new church, this entire passage may be proclaimed as one of the readings during Easter Time (Chapters II and III).

During the prayer of dedication of the new church (Chapters II and III), the bishop declares that the church is "God's dwelling-place with the human race" and prays that the poor find mercy, the oppressed attain freedom, and all be clothed with dignity "until they come exultant to the Jerusalem which is above."

When the bishop and priests anoint the altar and the walls of the new church (Chapters II and III), all may sing, "Behold God's dwelling with the human race. He will live with them and they will be his people, and God himself with them will be their God."

In the preface of the dedication of a newly built church (Chapter II), the bishop proclaims, "here is prefigured the image of the heavenly Jerusalem."

In the preface of the Mass for the dedication of a church already in use (Chapter III), the bishop prays that the Church may grow more as the Lord's own Body "till she reaches her fullness in the vision of peace, the heavenly city of Jerusalem." The same preface is used for the Mass celebrating the anniversary of the dedication of the church (Chapter VIII).

Psalm 84 provides several verses for one possible responsorial at the Mass of the dedication of a new altar in a previously dedicated church. They are paired with an antiphon from this passage of Revelation: either "Here God lives among his people" or "God who is with them will be their God" (Chapter IV).

This entire passage may be proclaimed as one of the readings at the Mass at the dedication of a church already in use (Chapter III) or when celebrating the anniversary of the dedication of the church (Chapter VIII) when either of these takes place during Easter Time. In the same Masses, one option for the responsorial is selected verses from Psalm 84, paired with a refrain from this passage: "Here God lives among his people."

In Your Heart
The book of Revelation envisions heaven as a new Jerusalem. When you think about this biblical city, what images come to mind? How would you connect the Jerusalem of biblical times with the future Jerusalem of Revelation?

What are the best aspects of the city where you live? What makes you proud to call it home? How does your own city help you envision heaven?

Your parish church is an image of the new Jerusalem. How does your parish community display the virtues of an ideal city? How does it prefigure the glory of heaven?

118. Revelation 21:9b-14

In the Bible

In his vision, John is carried toward a mountain where he sees the new Jerusalem. Its high wall has twelve gates, the gates have twelve angels and the inscribed names of the tribes of Israel. Three gates open on each of the four walls. The walls have twelve foundations on which are written the names of the apostles of the Lamb.

In the Liturgy

When the bishop and priests anoint the walls of the new church, they may apply sacred chrism to twelve or to four places (Chapters II and III). The numbers reflect the twelve gates and four walls of the new Jerusalem.

At the Mass of dedication of a newly built church (Chapter II), the preface for the eucharistic prayer praises God who "established the Church as a holy city, built upon the foundation of the Apostles."

The entire passage may be proclaimed as the first reading at the dedication of a church already in use (Chapter III) or on the anniversary of the dedication of the church (Chapter VIII), when either of these takes place in Easter Time.

In Your Heart
John envisions the new Jerusalem as a walled city of great
strength. Where do you feel safest? Why? How does that help
you envision the new Jerusalem?

The church is built upon the foundation of the apostles.
Who are the founders of your parish church? How does their
vision continue?

When you go to church, which door do you enter? Which
direction does it face? How does that door remind you of your
ancestors in the faith? How does it serve as a gateway from the
church to the world?

119. Revelation 21:23-24

In the Bible
In John's vision of the new Jerusalem, the glory of God is its
light, and its lamp is the lamb. It has no need of sun or moon.
Nations walk by the light of this city.

In the Liturgy
When the bishop dedicates a new church, he offers a special
prayer (Chapters II and III). He acclaims that the church is "a
City set high on a mountain for all to see, resplendent to every
eye with the unfading light of the Lamb."

In Your Heart
Think about all the lights you have needed over the past twenty-
four hours. Where did you need lights beyond the sun? Why?
How did light help you through your day?

How is your parish church a light for you? Who are the
people who represent the light of the Lamb of God?

How is your parish a light for others to see? How do you
shine the light of Christ on those who have not yet believed?

120. Revelation 22:13 and 1:8

In the Bible

In the first and last chapters of the last book of the Bible, John hears a proclamation of the one who is, who was, and who is to come, and sees a vision of Christ as an angel who declares, "I am the Alpha and the Omega, the first and the last, the beginning and the end."

In the Liturgy

When the bishop goes to the place where the foundation stone is to be laid for commencement of work on a new church, he offers a prayer (Chapter I). He prays to the Father, "Grant that he, whom you have established as the beginning and the end of all things, may be the origin, progress, and fulfillment of this work."

In Your Heart

How do you begin and end each day? Do you make Christ a part of your daily life? How?

As your new church is under construction, how has Christ been part of the beginning of this work? How are you praying for him to accompany its construction? How will the mission of Christ be fulfilled in this new church?

How has Christ been part of your life from the moment of your conception? How do you hope Christ will be your companion at the end of your days?

.